Cookbook for Girls

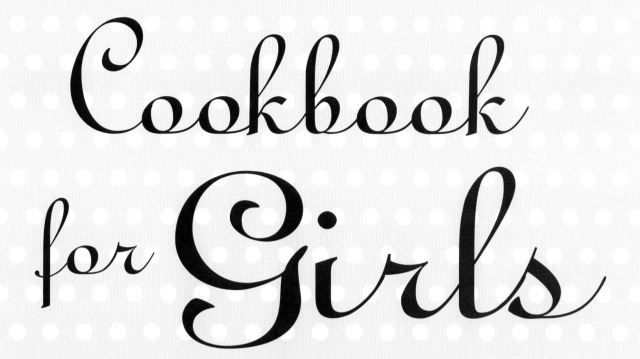

Written by Denise Smart
Photography by Howard Shooter

LONDON, NEW YORK, MUNICH,
MELBOURNE, AND DELHI

Project Editor Heather Scott
Senior Designer Lisa Crowe
Home Economist Denise Smart
Craft Designer/Stylist Suzie Harrison
Indexer Julia March
Brand Manager Lisa Lanzarini
Publishing Manager Simon Beecroft
Category Publisher Alex Allan
Print Production Amy Bennett
Production Editor Clare McLean
US Editor Margaret Parrish

First published in the United States in 2009
by DK Publishing, 375 Hudson Street
New York, New York 10014

09 10 11 12 13 10 9 8 7 6 5 4 3 2
GD114—12/08

Published in Great Britain by
Dorling Kindersley Limited.

ISBN: 978-0-7566-4500-7
Reproduced by Alta Image, UK
Printed and bound by Hung Hing, China

Acknowledgments
p. 119 (t, r) Tim Ridley © Dorling Kindersley; p. 121 (t, l), p. 123 (t, r) and p. 124 (t) © Dorling Kindersley; p. 123 (t, l) Andy Crawford © Dorling Kindersley.

The publisher would like to thank the photographer's assistant Ria Osborne for all her help, and the following girls for being fantastic hand models and trainee chefs: Eleanor Bullock, Hannah Moore, Elise Flatman, and Mykelia Hill.

Discover more at
www.dk.com

Contents

Introduction

This book is all about creating truly scrumptious food that you and your friends and family will love to eat. There are some old favorites as well as new ideas to inspire you to get in the kitchen and start cooking!

Getting started

1. Read the recipe thoroughly before you begin.
2. Wash your hands, tie your hair back (if necessary), and put on your apron.
3. Gather all the ingredients and equipment you need before you begin.
4. Start cooking!

Beef chow mein p. 48

Safe cooking

Cooking is lots of fun, but with heat and sharp objects around you must always take care to be safe and sensible.

- Use oven mitts when handling hot pans, trays, or bowls.
- Don't put hot pans or trays directly onto the work surface—use a heatproof trivet, mat, rack, or board.
- When you are stirring food on the stove, grip the handle firmly to steady the pan.
- When cooking on the stove, turn the pan handles to the side (away from the heat and the front) so that you are less likely to knock them over.
- Take extra care on any step where you see the warning triangle symbol.

Kitchen hygiene

After safety, cleanliness is the most important thing to be aware of in the kitchen. Here are a few simple hygiene rules for you to follow.

- Always wash your hands before you start cooking, and after handling raw meat.
- Wash all fruit and vegetables.
- Use separate cutting boards for meat and vegetables.
- Keep your cooking area clean and have a cloth handy to wipe up any spills.
- Store cooked and raw food separately.
- Always check the use-by date on all ingredients. Do not use them if the date has passed.
- Keep meat and fish in the refrigerator until you need them and always take care to cook them thoroughly.

Wash your hands after handling raw meat

Always wash fresh fruit and vegetables

How to use the recipes

There's a lot of information packed on each page. Use the key below to find out what each feature tells you, including how long a recipe takes to prepare and cook, and how many it serves.

Check here for quantity of servings and preparation and cooking times in minutes, unless otherwise stated.

This tells you which section the recipe is from.

Makes 16 Preparation 15 Cooking 70

Main meals

Cheesy potato skins

Crispy bacon and melted cheese make these potato skins a firm favorite. If you and your friends don't like bacon, substitute it with tuna or chicken or leave it out completely.

Ingredients

- 4 large baking potatoes
- oil for brushing
- 8 strips bacon
- ½ tsp (2.5 ml) paprika
- 2 oz (50 g) sharp Cheddar cheese, grated
- 2 oz (50 g) mozzarella cheese, grated
- 6 scallions, chopped

Dip:
- ½ cup (150 ml) sour cream
- 4 tsp (60 ml) fresh chives

Tools

- fork
- pastry brush
- cookie sheet
- knife
- cutting board
- wooden spoon
- frying pan
- 2 spoons
- small bowl

1 Preheat the oven to 400°F (200°C). Prick the potatoes with a fork and brush them with oil. Bake for 1 hour, until cooked. Cool slightly.

2 Cut up the bacon into small pieces. Place the bacon in a frying pan and dry fry, until lightly browned.

3 Cut the potatoes in half and scoop out the flesh with a spoon, leaving a thin layer. Cut each potato in half lengthwise to make boat shapes.

4 Place on a cookie sheet, season and sprinkle over a little paprika. Top with half of the bacon pieces. Mix together the cheeses and scallions and sprinkle over the potatoes. Top with the remaining bacon.

5 Return the potato skins to the oven until golden. Cool for 10 minutes. Mix together the dip ingredients and serve with the skins.

Top tip! Make sure the potatoes get really crispy in the oven—it will be worth the wait!

50 These easy-to-make filled potato skins are a delicious option for a party! 51

The intro tells you a bit about the dish.

Top tips provide useful suggestions and alternatives.

Collect all the ingredients and equipment before you start.

Step-by-step pictures and text guide you through the recipes.

This sentence gives you helpful hints about when to enjoy each dish.

Snacks

Serves 4 Preparation 10 Cooking 10

Red pepper hummous

This roasted red pepper hummous makes a perfect dip for snacking when served with toasted pitta or crudités. Alternatively, spread onto tortillas with some crumbled feta cheese for an easy wrap.

Ingredients

- 2 red peppers, deseeded and each cut into 4 pieces
- 15 oz (400 g) can chickpeas, drained and rinsed
- 2 cloves garlic, peeled
- 2 tbsp (30 ml) tahini (sesame seed paste)
- juice ½ lemon
- 3 tbsp (45 ml) olive oil
- a little paprika

Tools

- knife
- food processor
- plastic bag
- bowl

1 Place the red peppers under a hot broiler. Broil until the skins have blackened. Place in a plastic bag and when cool, peel off the blackened skin.

2 Place the skinless peppers with the remaining ingredients in a food processor and blend until smooth and creamy.

3 Transfer the hummous to a bowl and sprinkle with a little paprika. Serve with toasted pitta breads or vegetable crudités.

This healthy snack is great served with

Top tip!

Wait until the peppers are cool before you peel the skin off—you don't want burned fingers!

vegetable dippers like carrot and cucumber

Serves 4 Preparation 10 Cooking 6

Griddled fruit & honey

Ingredients

- 3 peaches
- 4 apricots
- 2 tbsp (30 ml) sugar
- 1/2 tsp (2.5 ml) ground cinnamon
- 1 cup (200 ml) Greek yogurt
- 2 tbsp (30 ml) clear honey

Tools

- knife
- cutting board
- 2 mixing bowls
- 2 metal spoons
- griddle pan
- tongs

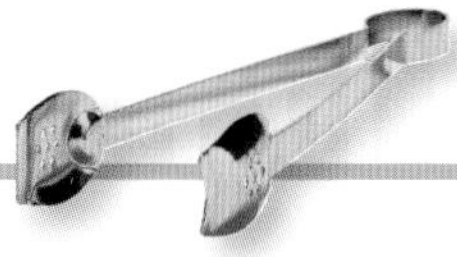

You will love this fruit griddled—it helps bring out the sweetness. If you don't have a griddle pan, place the fruit under a hot broiler.

1 Cut each peach in half and remove the pit. Then cut each half into quarters. Halve the apricots and remove the pits.

2 In a large bowl, mix together the sugar and cinnamon, then add the fruit. Toss to coat in the sugar mixture.

3 Preheat a griddle pan and add the peaches, flesh side down. Cook for 2 to 3 minutes. Add the apricots, and turn over the peaches. Cook until caramelized.

4 Meanwhile, place the yogurt in a bowl and pour over the honey. Stir to create a rippled effect. Serve the warmed griddled fruit with the yogurt and honey dip.

Slices of mango and pineapple

Top tip!

If you don't like Greek yogurt, try this with ice cream or crème fraîche.

are also delicious griddled

Cheese & pesto straws

Flavored with pesto and cheese, these light crisp straws are perfect for dipping.

These tasty cheese & pesto straws

Ingredients

- 1 1/2 cups (200 g) all-purpose flour
- 1/2 cup (125 g) chilled butter, cut into small cubes
- 1/2 cup (50 g) Gruyère or Cheddar cheese, finely grated
- 1/2 cup (50 g) Parmesan cheese, finely grated
- 1 whole medium egg, plus 1 yolk
- 2 tbsp (30 ml) pesto sauce (either red or green)

Tools

- strainer or sifter
- mixing bowl
- metal spoon
- rolling pin
- knife
- baking parchment
- cookie sheet
- cooling rack

1 Preheat the oven to 350°F (180°C). Sift the flour into a bowl with a pinch of salt. Add the butter and rub in until it looks like fine breadcrumbs.

2 Stir in 3/4 cup (75 g) of the cheeses. Beat together the egg and egg yolk and stir into the flour with the pesto sauce. Mix to a dough.

3 The mixture should be of the consistency where you can roll it into a ball.

4 Roll out on a lightly floured surface into a rectangle about 11 in (28 cm) x 9 in (23 cm). Cut in half down the longest length, then cut each into about 15 straws.

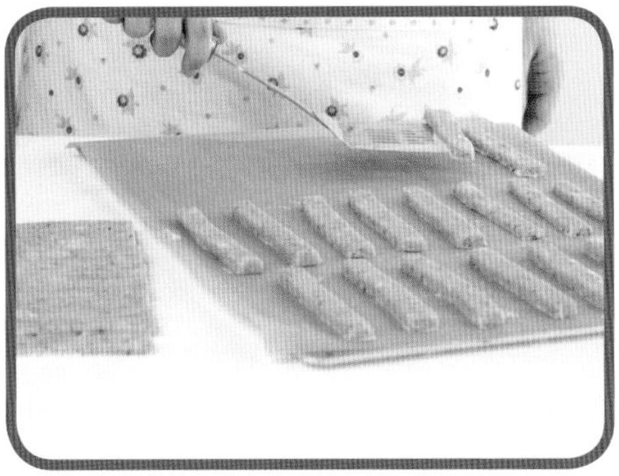

5 Line a cookie sheet with baking parchment. Transfer the straws to the cookie sheet, leaving a gap between each.

6 Sprinkle over the remaining cheese and chill for 15 minutes. Bake for 12 to 15 minutes. Cool for 5 minutes on the sheet, then transfer to a cooling rack.

Serves 4 Preparation 5 Cooking 4

Nachos & salsa

Make this quick tomato salsa and spoon over tortilla chips with cheese for a tasty snack.

Top tip!

Add some cooked diced chicken or kidney beans to make this snack more filling.

Ingredients

- 1 x 8 oz (200 g) bag plain tortilla chips
- 1/2 cup (50 g) mozzarella cheese, grated
- 1/2 cup (50 g) mature Cheddar cheese, grated

Salsa:

- 3 medium tomatoes
- 1/2 red onion, finely chopped
- 2 cloves garlic, crushed
- juice 1/2 lime
- 4 tbsp (60 ml) freshly chopped cilantro
- 1/2 tsp (2.5 ml) sugar
- 1 green chili, deseeded and chopped

Tools

- cutting board
- knife
- mixing bowl
- metal spoon
- cookie sheet

1 Cut the tomatoes in half and remove the seeds, then dice. Place in a bowl and stir in all the remaining salsa ingredients.

2 Place the nachos on a large cookie sheet or shallow ovenproof dish and spoon over the salsa.

3 Scatter over the cheese. Place under a preheated broiler for 3 to 4 minutes until the cheese has melted.

Nachos are a tasty Mexican snack made

Top tip!

Serve with sour cream and guacamole to dip your delicious nachos into.

from fried or baked corn tortillas

Serves 4 Preparation 10 Cooking 35

Spicy potato wedges

These spiced potato wedges can be eaten as a snack, served with a cooling sour cream and chive dip. Alternatively, they make a great accompaniment to the burgers on page 42.

Ingredients

- 3 medium baking potatoes, (about 1¼ lb or 650 g)
- 2 tbsp (30 ml) olive oil
- 1 tbsp (15 ml) paprika
- 2 tsp (10 ml) ground cumin
- 2 tsp (10 ml) dried mixed herbs
- ½ tsp (2.5 ml) cayenne pepper (optional)
- ½ tsp (2.5 ml) salt

Tools

- knife
- cutting board
- large saucepan
- mixing bowl
- metal spoon
- nonstick cookie sheet
- pastry brush

1 Preheat the oven to 400°F (200°C). Cut each potato into 8 wedges.

2 Bring a pan of water to the boil, add the potatoes, and simmer for 8 minutes. Drain and return to the pan. Allow to cool slightly.

3 In a bowl, mix together all the remaining ingredients; add the potatoes, and toss gently to coat in the spice mixture.

4 Place on a nonstick cookie sheet, skin side down, and brush with any remaining spice mixture. Cook for 20 to 25 minutes until golden brown.

These spicy potato wedges are a

Top tip!

Make sure the wedges get nice and crispy in the oven before taking them out.

healthy and delicious alternative to chips

Serves 4 Preparation 20 Cooking 5

Vegetable tempura

Ingredients

Peanut dipping sauce:
- 1 tbsp (15 ml) sesame seeds
- 2 tbsp (30 ml) smooth, unsalted peanut butter
- 1 tbsp (15 ml) dark soy sauce
- 1 tbsp (15 ml) rice wine vinegar
- 1 tbsp (15 ml) cold water

- 2 tsp (10 ml) sugar
- ½ tsp (2.5 ml) chili powder
- vegetable oil, for frying

Tempura batter:
- 1½ cups (200 g) self-rising flour
- 1 tsp (5 ml) corn starch

- 2 egg yolks
- 12 fl oz (350 ml) ice-cold water
- 1 lb (450 g) mixed vegetables

Tools

- saucepan
- wooden spoon
- 2 bowls
- whisk
- measuring cup
- chopstick
- saucepan
- slotted spoon

These vegetables are cooked in a light, crisp batter and served with dipping sauce. Choose a selection of your favorite vegetables.

1 Prepare the dip. Place the sesame seeds in a frying pan and cook over a moderate heat until lightly toasted.

2 Place the sesame seeds in a bowl and whisk in all the remaining dressing ingredients, until well combined and smooth.

3 Place the flour and corn starch in a bowl. Whisk the egg yolks with the chilled water. Add this to the mixture and mix with a chopstick. Mixture should be lumpy.

4 Fill a saucepan ⅓ full of oil and heat to a medium temperature. Dip the vegetables in the batter and fry them for 2 to 3 minutes. Remove with a slotted spoon.

These also taste delicious served

Top tip!

Button mushrooms, small cauliflower florets, zucchini, red pepper, or carrots cut into thin strips all work well in this recipe.

with sweet chili dipping sauce

Light meals

Serves 2 *Preparation* 40 *Cooking* 5

Bruschetta

Bruschetta is a tasty Italian starter or snack. It is traditionally made by piling ripe tomatoes onto toasted garlic bread.

Top tip!

Try adding some torn mozzarella, which can also be lightly toasted under a broiler.

Ingredients

- 4 x 1/2 in (2.5 cm) slices Italian-style bread such as ciabatta
- 3 medium ripe tomatoes
- 1 tbsp (15 ml) olive oil
- 6 basil leaves
- 1 clove garlic, peeled

Tools

- knife
- cutting board
- metal spoon
- strainer
- bowl
- griddle pan

1 Halve and deseed the tomatoes. Press the seeds through a strainer over a bowl, then discard the seeds. Dice the tomatoes and add to the bowl.

2 Add the olive oil, salt, and freshly ground black pepper. Leave to stand for 30 minutes. Roll up the basil leaves, chop finely, then add to the mixture.

3 Toast the bread on both sides, preferably in a griddle pan to create dark lines, or under a preheated broiler.

4 Rub the hot bread with the clove of garlic. Place each piece of bread on a plate and heap with the tomato mixture.

Use the freshest ingredients to make

these deliciously simple bruschetta

Serves 4 Preparation 15

Jewel salad

This colorful salad made with couscous and pretty pomegranate seeds makes a great accompaniment or a light meal.

Ingredients

- 1¼ cup (200 g) couscous
- 1¼ cup (300 ml) hot vegetable stock
- ½ lb (250 g) cherry tomatoes
- ½ cucumber
- 1 medium sized pomegranate
- 2 tbsp (30 ml) olive oil
- grated zest and juice 1 lemon
- 1 small red onion, thinly sliced
- 1¼ cup (200 g) feta cheese, crumbled
- large bunch (about 6 tbsp) freshly chopped mint

Tools

- 3 bowls
- measuring cup
- fork
- cutting board
- knife
- teaspoon
- wooden spoon

1 Place the couscous in a large bowl and pour over the hot stock and leave for 5 minutes until all the liquid has been absorbed. Allow to cool completely.

2 Cut the cherry tomatoes in half. Halve the cucumber lengthwise and scoop out the seeds with a teaspoon, then cut into pieces.

3 Cut the pomegranate in half, and hold one half over a bowl. Lightly tap the pomegranate with a wooden spoon, until the seeds fall into the bowl.

4 Stir the lemon juice, zest, and olive oil into the couscous. Add the tomatoes, cucumber, red onion, feta cheese, and mint, then stir in the pomegranate seeds.

Pomegranates are in

Top tip!
You can buy pomegranate seeds from the supermarket if you are in a hurry!

Serves 4 Preparation 10

Club sandwich

This club sandwich is made using ham, chicken, and cheese on toasted bread. However, you can use any combination of your favorite meats or cheeses.

This is a superdeluxe sandwich —

Ingredients

- 4 slices white bread
- 2 slices wholewheat bread
- 4 tbsp (60 ml) mayonnaise
- 1 tbsp (15 ml) lemon juice
- 1 cup (50 g) shredded iceberg lettuce
- 2 slices ham
- 2 slices Swiss or Cheddar cheese
- 1 tomato, sliced
- 2 oz (50 g) cooked chicken breast, shredded

Tools

- bread knife
- cutting board
- mixing bowl
- metal spoon
- toothpicks

1 Lightly toast the bread on both sides under a preheated moderate broiler or in a toaster. Cut off the crusts.

2 In a small bowl mix together the mayonnaise and lemon juice. Season to taste. Stir in the shredded lettuce.

3 Spread 2 slices of the white toast with half of the lettuce and mayonnaise mixture.

4 Place a slice of ham, then a slice of cheese on top of each. Top with the wholewheat bread, spread with the remaining lettuce and mayonnaise.

5 Add some slices of tomato and the chicken. Top with the remaining white toast.

6 Cut each sandwich into 4 triangles and secure each with a toothpick.

perfect for a luxurious lunch!

Serves 4 Preparation 10 Cooking 15

Chicken pasta salad

Ingredients

- 4 oz (125 g) pasta bows
- 2 tsp (10 ml) sunflower oil
- 1 tbsp (15 ml) medium curry paste
- 3 scallions, chopped
- 1 ripe mango

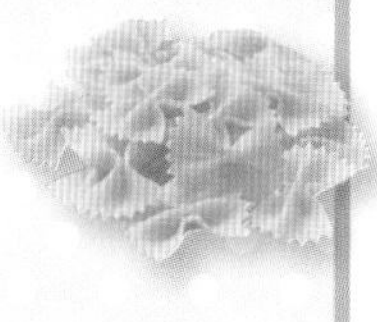

- juice 1/2 lemon
- 1/2 cup (100 ml) low fat yogurt
- 1/2 cup (100 ml) mayonnaise
- 12 oz (350 g) cooked chicken breast, diced
- 2 tbsp (30 ml) freshly chopped cilantro
- 1 cup (150 g) mixed red and green grapes, halved

Tools

- large saucepan
- small frying pan
- wooden spoon
- knife
- mixing bowl

This mildly spiced pasta and chicken salad makes a perfect light lunch or is ideal for a school lunchbox.

1 Bring a large pan of lightly salted water to the boil. Add the pasta and cook according to package instructions. Drain and rinse under cold running water.

2 Meanwhile, in a small frying pan heat the oil, add the curry paste and scallions, and cook for 2 minutes. Leave to cool.

3 Cut away the two sides of the mango, close to the pit. Cut the flesh into criss-cross patterns, press each half inside out, and carefully cut off the cubes.

4 Place the spice mixture in a bowl and stir in the lemon juice, yogurt, mayonnaise, and cilantro. Add the chicken, mango, and grapes. Chill until ready to eat.

The spicy and sweet flavors in

Top tip!

If you are a vegetarian, just leave out the chicken. Try adding tofu instead.

this pasta salad are a tasty combination

Serves 4 Preparation 5 Cooking 15

Potato salad

This simple potato salad substitutes traditional mayonnaise for a lighter creamy sauce, flavored with chives.

Top tip!
If you like hot and spicy flavors, try adding 1 tbsp (15 ml) of horseradish sauce.

Ingredients

- $1\frac{1}{4}$ lb (500g) baby new potatoes
- 3 tbsp (45 ml) reduced fat crème fraîche
- 3 tbsp (45 ml) low fat yogurt
- 2 tbsp (30 ml) freshly chopped chives

Tools

- knife
- cutting board
- saucepan
- 2 mixing bowls
- metal spoon

1 Wash and cut any larger potatoes in half.

2 Cook in a pan of lightly salted boiling water for 12 to 15 minutes. Drain and allow to cool. Place in a bowl.

3 In a small bowl, mix together the crème fraîche, yogurt, and fresh chives.

4 Gently stir the chive mixture into the potatoes. Season to taste. Keep refrigerated until ready to serve.

This is a healthier version of

Top tip!

Make sure the potatoes are cool, or you will have a warm potato salad!

an old favorite. Perfect for picnics!

Serves 4 Preparation 10 Cooking 5

Green salad

This salad makes a great accompaniment to grilled fish or chicken. You can add your own favorite vegetables—just remember to keep them green!

Ingredients

- 1 cup (100 g) green beans, trimmed and halved
- $1\frac{1}{2}$ cups (100 g) tenderstem broccoli
- $1\frac{1}{2}$ cups (100 g) fresh peas
- 3 cups (150 g) mixed leaves, e.g., baby spinach, arugula, and watercress

Dressing:
- 2 tbsp (30 ml) white wine vinegar
- 2 tbsp (30 ml) extra virgin olive oil
- 1 tbsp (15 ml) lemon juice
- 1 tsp (5 ml) clear honey
- 1 tsp (5 ml) pesto sauce

Tools

- saucepan
- small mixing bowl
- whisk
- large serving bowl
- measuring cup

1 Add the green beans to a pan of boiling water for 2 minutes. Then add the broccoli and peas and simmer for 3 minutes, and then strain*.

2 Make the dressing. Place all the ingredients in a bowl, season with salt and a little freshly ground black pepper, and whisk until combined.

3 Place the salad greens in a bowl and place the vegetables on top. Drizzle the dressing over the salad and toss together. Serve immediately.

This superhealthy salad is packed

Top tip!

*Once the vegetables are cooked, run them under cold water so they stop cooking and retain their color.

with vitamins and minerals!

Makes 12 Preparation 15 Cooking 15

Veggie spring rolls

These crispy spring rolls filled with vegetables are an easy and delicious snack. Serve with sweet chili dipping sauce or soy sauce if you prefer.

Ingredients

- 1¼ cup (100 g) beansprouts
- ¾ cup (50 g) cabbage, shredded
- 1 carrot, cut into thin strips
- ½ red pepper, deseeded and thinly sliced
- 6 scallions, thinly sliced
- 1 clove garlic, crushed
- 1 in (2.5 cm) piece root ginger, peeled and grated
- 1 tbsp (15 ml) dark soy sauce
- 6 sheets filo pastry
- 2 tbsp (25 g) melted butter

Tools

- mixing bowl
- wooden spoon
- cutting board
- knife
- small bowl
- pastry brush
- cookie sheet

1 Preheat the oven to 375°F (190°C). In a large bowl, mix together all the ingredients, except the filo pastry and butter.

2 Place the sheets of pastry on top of each other and cut in half.

3 Place 1 sheet of the pastry on a board and brush the edges with a little of the melted butter. Place some of the filling on the bottom edge.

Serve these as a starter at a dinner

4 Roll up, folding the ends over. Repeat with remaining pastry and filling.

5 Place on a cookie sheet and brush with butter. Bake for 12 to 15 minutes until golden. Serve with sweet chili dipping sauce.

Top tip!

You could try using sweetcorn, peas, or mushrooms if you prefer these fillings.

party, or as a midafternoon snack!

Serves 4 Preparation 10 Cooking 34

Baked eggs

You will love these baked eggs, cooked in a rich tomato and pepper sauce. Serve with warmed tortillas or crusty bread for a light lunch or breakfast.

Ingredients

- 1 tbsp (15 ml) olive oil
- 1 small onion, chopped
- 1 clove garlic, crushed
- 1 mild green chili, deseeded and finely chopped (optional)
- 1 small green pepper, deseeded and cut into thin strips

- 1 small red pepper, deseeded and cut into thin strips
- 15 oz (400 g) can chopped tomatoes

- 2 tbsp (30 ml) ketchup
- 4 eggs
- a little paprika

Tools

- medium saucepan
- wooden spoon
- 2 double, 4 individual, or one large ovenproof dish

1 Preheat the oven to 350°F (180°C). Heat the oil in a medium pan and add the onion, garlic, chili, and peppers. Cook for 10 to 15 minutes.

2 Stir in the tomatoes and ketchup and season with salt and black pepper. Bring to the boil, then simmer for 5 minutes until thickened.

3 Spoon the mixture into some ovenproof dishes. Make 4 dips and break an egg into each. Place in the oven and bake for 12 to 14 minutes, until just set.

This recipe is based on a traditional

Top tip!

Serve sprinkled with a little paprika, and with warmed flour tortillas.

Mexican recipe called "huevos rancheros"

Main meals

Serves 4 *Preparation* 40 *Cooking* 14

BBQ chicken skewers

These bite-sized skewers are a tasty option. Make up double quantities of the sauce and use half for dipping if you like.

Ingredients

- 12 skinless, boneless chicken thighs
- 1 red and 1 yellow pepper, deseeded and cut into chunks

Barbecue sauce:
- 6 tbsp (90 ml) ketchup
- 2 tbsp (30 ml) maple syrup or honey
- 2 tbsp (30 ml) dark soy sauce
- grated rind and juice 1 lime
- 2 tsp (10 ml) freshly grated ginger
- 2 tbsp (30 ml) soft brown sugar

Tools

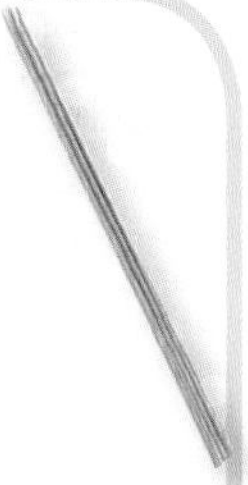

- small saucepan
- wooden spoon
- cutting board
- knife
- mixing bowl
- small wooden skewers (soaked in water for 30 minutes)
- pastry brush

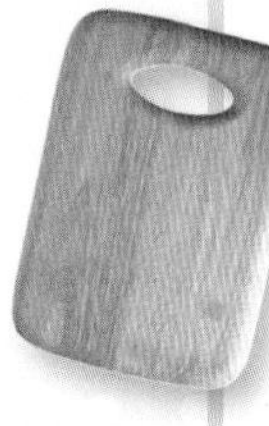

1 Place all the ingredients for the sauce in a small pan, bring to the boil, then simmer for 2 minutes, stirring until the sugar has dissolved. Allow to cool.

2 Cut each chicken thigh into 2 to 3 pieces. Place the cooled sauce in a large bowl.

3 Add the chicken, stir to coat, then leave to marinate for about 30 minutes.

These skewers are ideal served

4 Thread 2 to 3 pieces of chicken onto wooden skewers with pieces of red and yellow pepper. Repeat until all the chicken and peppers have been used up.

5 Line the base of a broiler pan with foil, then broil for 10 to 12 minutes, turning occasionally and brushing with the sauce, until the chicken is thoroughly cooked.

Top tip!

Remember to soak the wooden skewers in water for 30 minutes, to keep them from burning.

with rice or a green salad

Serves 4 Preparation 45 Cooking 9

Cream cheese burgers

These burgers have a surprise cream cheese, herb, and garlic filling. Serve in bread rolls with salad or with potato wedges.

These unusual burgers are delicious

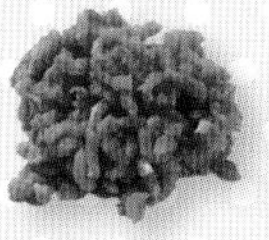

Ingredients

Burgers:
- $1\frac{1}{2}$ lb (675 g) lean ground beef
- 1 small onion, finely chopped
- 4 tbsp (60 ml) freshly chopped parsley

Cream cheese filling:
- 3 oz (75 g) soft cream cheese
- 1 clove garlic, crushed (optional)
- 2 tbsp (30 ml) freshly chopped chives
- little oil for brushing

Tools

- large bowl
- wooden spoon
- small bowl
- pastry brush
- flipper

1 In a large bowl, mix together all the ingredients for the burgers, with a little salt and freshly ground black pepper.

2 Divide into 8 equal portions and flatten into rounds.

Top tip!

This recipe works equally well by substituting the beef for ground chicken or turkey.

3 In a small bowl, mix together the cream cheese, garlic, and chives. Place a quarter of the mixture onto 4 of the burger rounds.

4 Place the other 4 burgers rounds on top and pinch together the edges. Mold into 4 burgers. Chill for 30 minutes.

5 Brush the burgers with a little oil and broil for 8 to 9 minutes on each side, until thoroughly cooked through. Serve in bread rolls with salad.

and much tastier than store-bought ones

Serves 4 Preparation 5 Cooking 32

Ingredients

- 1 tsp (5 ml) sunflower oil
- 4 oz (100 g) chorizo sausage, skin removed and chopped
- 1 onion, chopped
- 3 skinless chicken breasts, cubed

- 1¼ cups (225 g) easy-cook long grain rice
- 14 oz (400 g) can chopped tomatoes
- 1¾ cups (450 ml) hot chicken stock
- 1 tsp (5 ml) dried mixed herbs
- 1 red and green pepper, deseeded and cubed
- ⅓ cup (50 g) frozen peas
- 6 scallions, chopped

Tools

- large saucepan
- wooden spoon
- heatproof measuring cup

Jambalaya

This lightly spiced Cajun rice dish originated in Louisiana. The recipe can be easily adapted by adding your favorite vegetables or tofu.

1 Heat the oil in a large pan. Add the chorizo and onion and cook for 2 to 3 minutes, until the paprika oil from the chorizo is released.

2 Add the chicken and cook for 3 to 4 minutes until lightly browned on all sides. Stir in the rice until coated in the oil.

3 Add the tomatoes, stock, and herbs. Cover and simmer for 15 minutes, stirring occasionally.

4 Add the peppers, peas, and scallions and cook, covered for a further 10 minutes, until the rice is tender and most of the liquid has been absorbed.

For a spicier taste add 1 tsp of hot chili

powder or a dash of Tabasco sauce

Makes 24 Preparation 20 Cooking 9

Mini fish cakes

Serve these bite-sized fish cakes on toothpicks to make them easier to dip into the creamy lemon mayonnaise.

Use the discarded potato on page 50

Ingredients

Fish cakes:
- 14 oz (400 g) fresh salmon fillets
- 3 cups (400 g) cooked potato (use discarded potato from p. 50)
- 1/3 cup frozen peas, defrosted
- 1 1/4 cups (150 g) fresh bread crumbs
- 4 tbsp (60 ml) chopped fresh parsley
- 2 eggs, beaten
- sunflower oil for frying

Lemon mayonnaise:
- 1 cup (250 ml) low-fat mayonnaise
- grated zest and juice 1/2 lemon

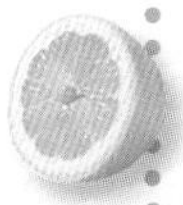

Tools

- medium saucepan or frying pan with lid
- 4 mixing bowls
- 3 metal spoons
- plate
- nonstick frying pan
- spatula

1 Place the fish in the pan. Add a little water, and bring to the boil. Cover and cook for 5 to 6 minutes. Allow to cool, then flake, removing any skin and bones.

2 Place the potato, peas, and salmon in a bowl. Mix gently until combined and season to taste.

3 Mix the bread crumbs with the parsley and place on a plate.

4 Place a heaped teaspoon of the salmon mixture in your hands, roll into a ball, then flatten. Dip into the egg, then coat in the bread crumb mixture.

5 Heat a little oil in a frying pan and shallow fry the fish cakes for 2 to 3 minutes each side until golden brown.

6 Mix together the mayonnaise with the lemon zest and juice. Transfer to a bowl. Serve the fish cakes warm or cold on toothpicks with the dip.

to make these scrumptious fish cakes

Serves 4 Preparation 15 Cooking 14

Beef chow mein

"Chow mein" means stir-fried noodles in Chinese Mandarin. You can add whatever you like. Try fish, meat, tofu, shrimp, or vegetables.

To be totally authentic, try using

Ingredients

- 1 clove garlic, crushed
- 1 in (2.5 cm) piece ginger root, peeled and grated
- 1 tbsp (15 ml) light soy sauce
- 1 tbsp (15 ml) rice wine vinegar
- $\frac{3}{4}$ lb (350 g) beef steak, (e.g., rump) thinly sliced
- 8 oz (about 6 cups, or 225 g) dried egg noodles
- 1 tbsp (15 ml) sunflower oil
- $\frac{3}{4}$ cup (75 g) snow peas, halved
- $1\frac{1}{2}$ cups (100 g) small broccoli florets
- 3 scallions, sliced
- 1 red pepper, deseeded and thinly sliced
- $1\frac{1}{4}$ cup (100 g) bean sprouts
- 2 tbsp (30 ml) oyster sauce
- 2 tsp (10 ml) toasted sesame oil

Tools

- mixing bowl
- metal spoon
- saucepan
- wooden spoon
- wok/frying pan

1 In a bowl, mix together the garlic, ginger, soy sauce, and rice wine vinegar. Add the sliced beef and stir, then leave to marinate for 10 minutes.

2 Meanwhile, cook the egg noodles. Place in a pan of boiling water and cook for 4 minutes, drain well, and return to the pan to keep warm.

3 Heat the sunflower oil in a large wok or frying pan. Add the beef and stir fry for 4 to 5 minutes until browned.

4 Add the snow peas, broccoli, scallions, and pepper. Stir fry for 2 to 3 minutes.

5 Add the noodles, bean sprouts, oyster sauce, and sesame oil, then stir fry for a further 2 minutes.

chopsticks to eat this Asian dish

Makes 16 Preparation 15 Cooking 70

Cheesy potato skins

Crispy bacon and melted cheese make these potato skins a firm favorite. If you and your friends don't like bacon, substitute it with tuna or chicken or leave it out completely.

Ingredients

- 4 large baking potatoes
- oil for brushing
- 8 strips bacon
- ½ tsp (2.5 ml) paprika
- 2 oz (50 g) sharp Cheddar cheese, grated
- 2 oz (50 g) mozzarella cheese, grated
- 6 scallions, chopped

Dip:

- ½ cup (150 ml) sour cream
- 4 tsp (60 ml) fresh chives

Tools

- fork
- pastry brush
- cookie sheet
- knife
- cutting board
- wooden spoon
- frying pan
- 2 spoons
- small bowl

1 Preheat the oven to 400°F (200°C). Prick the potatoes with a fork and brush them with oil. Bake for 1 hour, until cooked. Cool slightly.

2 Cut up the bacon into small pieces. Place the bacon in a frying pan and dry fry, until lightly browned.

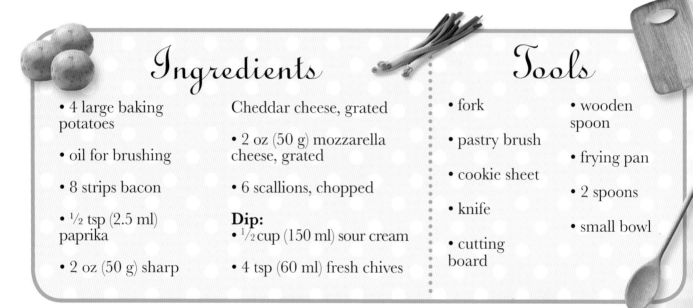

3 Cut the potatoes in half and scoop out the flesh with a spoon, leaving a thin layer. Cut each potato in half lengthwise to make boat shapes.

These easy-to-make filled potato skins

4 Place on a cookie sheet, season and sprinkle over a little paprika. Top with half of the bacon pieces. Mix together the cheeses and scallions and sprinkle over the potatoes. Top with the remaining bacon.

5 Return the potato skins to the oven until golden. Cool for 10 minutes. Mix together the dip ingredients and serve with the skins.

Top tip!

Make sure the potatoes get really crispy in the oven—it will be worth the wait!

are a delicious option for a party!

Serves 4 Preparation 15 Cooking 39

Butternut squash soup

This substantial soup is made from roasted butternut squash, but you could try it with pumpkin instead if you prefer.

This wholesome, warming soup

Ingredients

- $2\frac{1}{4}$ lb (1 kg) butternut squash
- 1 tbsp (15 ml) vegetable oil
- 1 onion, chopped
- $2\frac{1}{2}$ cups (600 ml) hot vegetable stock

- 2 tbsp (30 ml) honey

To serve:
French stick, Gruyère or Swiss cheese, and freshly chopped parsley

Tools

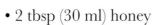

- knife
- 3 spoons
- cutting board
- vegetable peeler
- cookie sheet
- measuring cup
- food processor
- saucepan

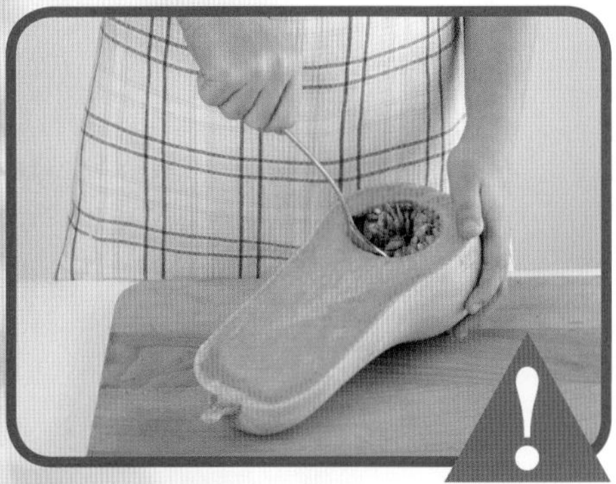

1 Preheat the oven to 400°F (200°C). Cut the butternut squash in half lengthwise, then, using a spoon, scoop out the seeds and pith.

2 Cut into large chunks, then, using a peeler, remove the skin. Cut these into 1 in (2.5 cm) cubes.

3 Place on a cookie sheet, season with salt and freshly ground black pepper, then drizzle over the oil. Roast for 20 minutes, then remove from the oven.

4 Add the onion and stir. Return to the oven and cook for a further 15 minutes.

5 Place the butternut squash and onion in a food processor with half of the stock and blend until smooth.

6 Place the purée in a saucepan with the remaining stock and honey. Simmer for 3 to 4 minutes. Serve with slices of toasted French stick, cheese, and parsley.

is perfect for a cold day

Serves 4 Preparation 20 Cooking 80

Sweet potato lasagne

This lasagne is lighter than a traditional lasagne. Ricotta cheese mixed with fresh basil replaces the traditional béchamel sauce.

Ingredients

- 4 medium tomatoes, quartered
- 1 red onion, cut into 8 wedges
- 3 sweet potatoes, (about 1 lb/ 450 g), peeled and thickly sliced
- 2 zucchinis, sliced
- 1 red pepper, deseeded and cubed
- 1 yellow pepper, deseeded and cubed

- 1 tbsp (15 ml) olive oil
- 1lb (500 g) ricotta cheese
- 3 tbsp (45 ml) freshly chopped basil
- 4 oz (100 g) Cheddar cheese, grated
- 4 fl oz (100 ml) heavy cream
- 1 medium egg, beaten
- 8 sheets fresh lasagne (about 4 oz/125 g)

Tools

- cutting board
- knife
- 3 mixing bowls
- roasting pan
- metal spoon
- large ovenproof dish

1 Preheat the oven to 350°F (180°C). Place all the vegetables in a bowl and add the olive oil. Season with salt and freshly ground black pepper.

2 Place the vegetables in a roasting pan. Cook for 40 minutes, stirring occasionally until tender.

3 Meanwhile, in a bowl combine the ricotta with the cream, basil, half the Chedder cheese, and the egg.

It might take a while to cut up all the

4 Arrange half the vegetables in the bottom of an ovenproof dish, place half the lasagne sheets over the top, then spoon over half the ricotta mixture.

5 Repeat once more, finishing with a layer of the cheese mixture. Sprinkle over the remaining cheese and bake for 35 to 40 minutes until golden and bubbling.

Top tip!

Use fresh lasagne sheets since there is no sauce for dried sheets to soak up.

vegetables so get friends or family to help!

Serves 4 Preparation 80 Cooking 20

Pizza squares

There will certainly be a topping to please everyone in this recipe, which makes 2 large pizzas. Why not top one with meat toppings and one with vegetarian toppings?

Top tip!

Try toppings like peppers, pineapple, ham, pepperoni, red onion, sweetcorn, or tomatoes.

These pick-and-mix pizzas allow you

Ingredients

Dough:
- $\frac{1}{2}$ tsp (2.5 ml) sugar
- 1 tsp (5 ml) active dried yeast
- 12 fl oz (350 ml) lukewarm water
- 1 tsp (5 ml) salt
- $3\frac{3}{4}$ cups (500 g) white bread flour
- 1 tbsp (15 ml) olive oil

Tomato sauce:
- 1 cup (300 ml) tomato sauce or purée
- 2 tbsp (30 ml) tomato paste
- $\frac{1}{2}$ tsp (2.5 ml) sugar
- 1 tsp (5 ml) dried mixed herbs
- 8 oz (200 g) grated mozzarella cheese

Tools

- mixing bowl
- metal spoon
- saucepan
- 2 cookie sheets
- strainer
- knife
- damp cloth
- wooden spoon
- rolling pin

1 Put the sugar, yeast, and water in a bowl, mix and leave for 5 minutes. In another bowl, sift the flour and salt, then add the oil and the yeast mixture.

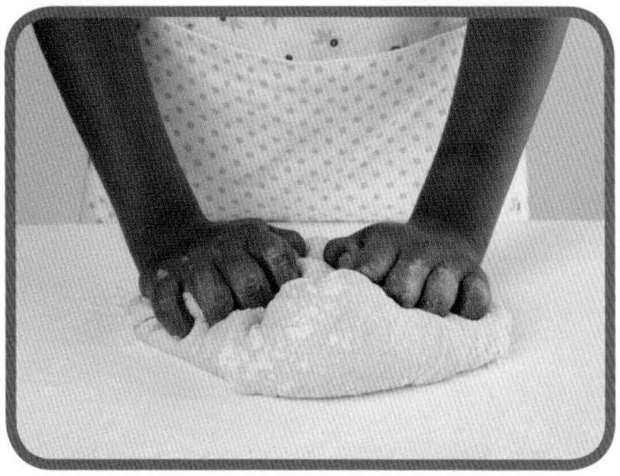

2 Stir with a knife to form a dough then knead for 4 to 5 minutes. Place in a bowl, cover with a clean damp cloth and leave in a warm place for 1 hour.

3 Meanwhile, make the tomato sauce. Place all the ingredients in a small pan and simmer gently for 5 minutes, allow to cool.

4 Preheat the oven to 450°F (220°C). Using a floured hand, punch the dough to knock out the air, then knead lightly on a floured surface.

5 Divide the dough in half, then roll out each into a rectangle on the cookie sheets. Spoon the tomato sauce over, then sprinkle with the cheese.

6 Turn one into a meat pizza and one into a vegetarian pizza. Bake for 15 minutes until golden, before cutting each into squares.

to create your own taste sensation!

Desserts

Serves 4 Preparation 20 Freezing 5h

Blueberry ice cream

This ice cream is so simple to make! Just mix all the prepared ingredients together and freeze.

Cut into rectangles and serve between

Ingredients

- 2½ cups (300 g) fresh blueberries
- 2 tbsp (30 ml) sugar
- grated zest and juice 1 unwaxed lemon
- 1¼ cups (300 ml) heavy cream
- 16 o… bio m…
- 2 t… con…

…ls

- large mixing bowl
- electric or hand whisk
- freezerproof container
- …her
- fork

1 Place the blueberries in a pan with the sugar and lemon zest and juice. Bring to the boil, then simmer for 4 to 5 minutes until the berries burst.

2 Remove from the heat and press through a fine sieve into a bowl, to make a glossy purple sauce. Leave to cool.

Top tip!

Place in the fridge for 15 minutes before serving to soften slightly.

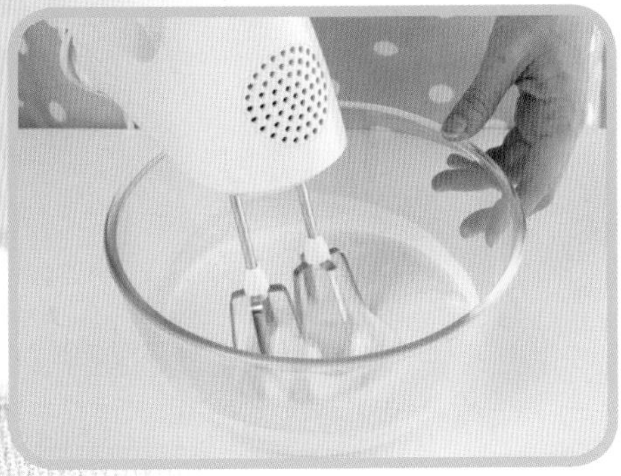

3 Place the cream in a large bowl and with an electric or hand whisk, lightly whip until just starting to thicken.

4 Using a metal spoon, fold in the yogurt and confectioners' sugar until well combined and smooth, then stir in the blueberry sauce.

5 Transfer to a freezerproof container with a lid. Place in freezer for 4 to 5 hours until frozen. Remove every hour and break up the ice crystals with a fork.

wafers for a sophisticated treat!

Makes 4 Preparation 5 Setting 3h

Very berry gelatin

These individual desserts are made using a mixture of frozen berries. Alternatively, you could just use one type of berry, such as frozen raspberries or blueberries.

Ingredients

- 5 oz (135 g) packet of raspberry or black currant flavor gelatin
- $1\frac{1}{4}$ cups (150 g) mixed frozen berries

Tools

- heatproof measuring cup
- spoon
- gelatin molds

1 Place the gelatin into a measuring cup and pour over $1\frac{1}{4}$ cups (300 ml) boiling water. Stir until the gelatin has dissolved.

2 Stir the fruit into the measuring cup. Top off with cold water to make $2\frac{1}{2}$ cups (600 ml), if necessary.

3 Spoon the mixtures between one large gelatin mold or four individual molds and place in the fridge for about 3 hours until set.

Make sure you leave enough time

Top tip!

Using frozen berries prevents them from floating to the top.

to let these yummy desserts set!

Makes 4 Preparation 15 Cooking 15

Apple crumble sundae

Layers of apple, crunchy crumble, toffee sauce, and ice cream are layered up in tall glasses to make a delicious sundae, which is a variation on an old favorite.

Top tip!

Use good quality vanilla ice cream—your sundaes won't be as delicious if you don't!

Serve these sundaes in traditional

Ingredients

Crumble mixture:
- 3/4 cup (100 g) flour
- 2 oz (50 g) butter, diced
- 1/4 cup (50 g) raw sugar

Apple compote:
- 3 cooking apples, peeled, cored, and chopped
- 1/4 cup (50 g) sugar
- juice 1/2 lemon
- 8 tbsp (90 ml) cold fudge sauce (see page 70) or ready-made toffee sauce
- 8 scoops vanilla ice cream

Tools

- medium bowl
- cookie sheet
- baking parchment
- medium saucepan
- wooden spoon
- fork

1 Place the flour and butter in a bowl and rub them together with your fingertips until the mixture resembles fine bread crumbs. Stir in the sugar.

2 Preheat the oven to 400°F (200°C). Line a cookie sheet with baking parchment, and pour the mixture on top. Cook for 8 to 10 minutes until golden.

3 Meanwhile, place the apples, sugar, and lemon juice in a medium pan. Cover and cook over a gentle heat for 12 to 15 minutes, stirring occasionally.

4 Leave the apple compote to cool with the lid off. Using your fingers or a fork, break up the cooled crumble topping.

5 Layer each sundae glass with apple compote, crumble, ice cream, and toffee sauce and serve with long spoons.

Top tip!

Serve warm with ice cream to get a deliciously different dessert!

sundae glasses for a retro feel

Serves 8 Preparation 10 Setting 2h

Raspberry cheesecake

This fruity cheesecake is so simple to make. The gelatin adds flavor and also sets the cheesecake.

Light, creamy, and delicious, this

Ingredients

- 3 oz (75 g) unsalted butter
- 6 oz (150 g) graham crackers (1¾ cups crushed)
- 5 oz (135 g) packet of raspberry flavor gelatin
- 1 cup (200 ml) evaporated milk, chilled
- 1 cup (200 g) soft cream cheese
- 1 cup (100 g) raspberries
- a few raspberries for decoration

Tools

- 8 in (20 cm) round loose-bottomed cake pan
- baking parchment
- food bag
- rolling pin
- saucepan
- 3 metal spoons
- heatproof measuring cup
- large bowl
- electric whisk

1 Line the base of an 8 in (20 cm) round loose-bottomed cake pan with baking parchment.

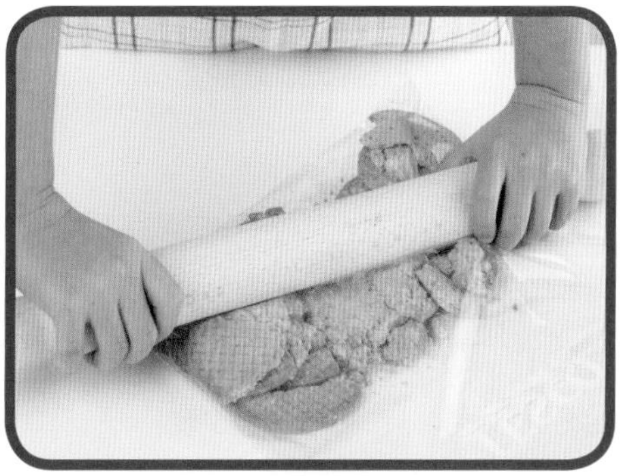

2 Place the crackers in a food bag and crush with a rolling pin (or you can do this in a food processor).

3 Melt the butter in a saucepan and stir in the crushed crackers. Press into the pan and chill.

4 In a measuring cup, put the gelatin in 4 fl oz (100 ml) of boiling water, and stir until dissolved.

5 In a large bowl, whisk the milk until light and fluffy and doubled in volume. Whisk in the cream cheese, until the mixture is smooth. Whisk in the gelatin.

6 Roughly chop the raspberries and stir into the mixture. Pour over the cracker base and leave to chill for 2 hours. Serve decorated with extra raspberries.

cheesecake is heavenly to eat

Serves 4 Preparation 5 Cooking 7

Fruit & choc fondue

This dessert is so simple to make. Serve the fruit on toothpicks to make dipping easier.

Ingredients

- 2 cups (250 g) mixed fruit
- 8 oz (200 g) good quality white chocolate, roughly chopped
- $^3/_4$ cup (150 ml) heavy cream
- 2 oz (50 g) unsalted butter, diced
- 1 tsp (5 ml) vanilla extract

Tools

- knife
- cutting board
- wooden spoon
- bowl
- saucepan

1 Prepare the fruit if necessary, remove the stalks from the strawberries and cut the banana into bite-sized pieces. Place on toothpicks.

2 Place the chocolate, cream, butter, and vanilla extract in a small bowl, set over a pan of simmering water. Heat gently for 5 to 7 minutes, stirring occasionally until the mixture is smooth.

 You can use marshmallows instead of fruit

Makes 8 Preparation 20 Freezing 6h

Mango pops

These fruity ice pops are made from pure fruit purée. Decorate with a little melted chocolate and sprinkles.

Ingredients

- 2 large ripe mangoes
- 2 tbsp (30 ml) confectioners' sugar
- juice 1 lime
- 6 oz (150 g) dark or milk chocolate, broken into pieces
- 1/3 cup (50 g) sprinkles

Tools

- knife
- cutting board
- food processor
- ice-pop molds and sticks

1 Copy step 3 on page 28. Place the mango in a food processor with the confectioners' sugar and lime juice and blend to a smooth purée.

2 Pour into 8 molds and put the sticks in. Freeze for 6 hours. Melt the chocolate and dip the pops in, then dip in the sprinkles. Keep in the freezer until ready to serve.

These fruity pops are a healthy treat

Serves 4 Preparation 20 Cooking 15

Banana fritters

These bananas are cooked in a light batter, coated with sesame seeds, and served with a delicious warm fudge sauce. For extra indulgence, add a scoop of vanilla ice cream.

Ingredients

- 4 bananas, peeled and each cut into 4 pieces
- sunflower oil for frying

Fudge sauce:
- 3 oz (75 g) unsalted butter
- 3/4 cup (150 g) light soft brown sugar
- 2/3 cup (150 ml) cream
- 1 tbsp (15 ml) dark corn syrup

Batter:
- 1 cup (125 g) self-rising flour
- 2 tbsp (30 ml) sugar
- 3/4 cup (175 ml) milk
- 4 tbsp (60 ml) sesame seeds

Tools

- large saucepan
- wooden spoon
- large bowl
- large metal spoon
- teaspoon
- slotted spoon
- paper towels

1 Place all the fudge sauce ingredients in a pan and cook gently for 2 to 3 minutes. Stirring continuously, bring to the boil for 3 minutes, until thickened.

2 Leave in the pan to cool slightly. Meanwhile, heat a pan 1/3 of the volume full of oil, until a piece of bread goes golden brown when dropped in.

3 Mix all the batter ingredients together in a large bowl, reserving 2 tbsp (30 ml) of the sesame seeds. Add the bananas and turn to coat in the batter.

These banana fritters are a

4 Using a slotted spoon, and holding over the bowl, remove the bananas, then sprinkle with some of the reserved sesame seeds.

5 Fry the banana in batches, in the oil for 3 to 4 minutes until golden brown. Remove and drain on paper towels. Serve immediately with the fudge sauce.

Top tip!

Eat these as soon as they are cooked since the batter will become soggy if you leave them.

quick and delicious dessert

Makes 15 Preparation 10 Cooking 60

Strawberry meringues

These delicious pretty meringues are crisp on the outside and soft in the middle. Fill with lightly whipped cream and sliced strawberries.

Top tip!
You can make vanilla sugar by leaving a vanilla pod in a jar of sugar.

Unfilled meringues can be kept in an

Ingredients

- 2 large egg whites
- 1/2 cup (100 g) superfine sugar
- 1/2 cup (150 ml) heavy cream
- 1 tbsp (15 ml) vanilla sugar
- 12 small strawberries, sliced

Tools

- 2 large cookie sheets
- baking parchment
- large mixing bowl
- electric whisk
- tablespoon
- teaspoon

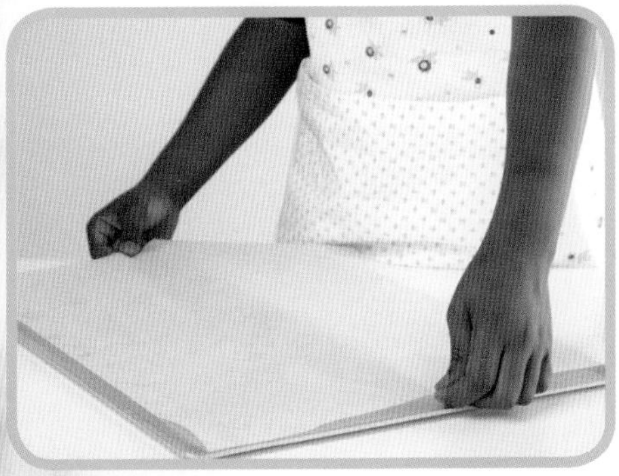

1 Preheat the oven to 225°F (110°C). Lightly grease 2 large cookie sheets and line with baking parchment.

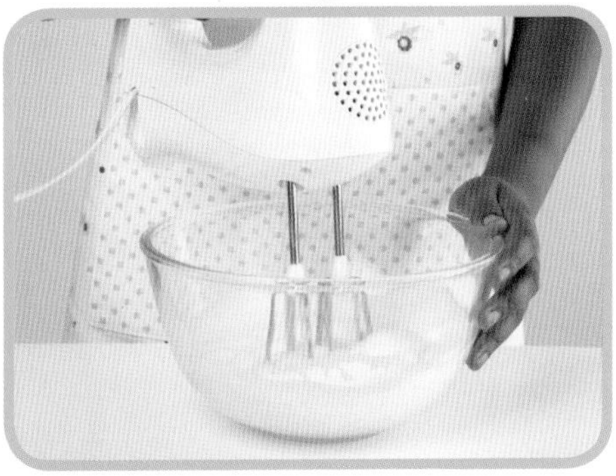

2 Place the egg whites into a large, spotlessly clean mixing bowl and whisk them until they form stiff peaks.

3 Add the sugar a tablespoon at a time, whisking well after each addition, until the mixture is smooth, thick, and glossy.

4 Place heaped teaspoons of the mixture, spaced a little apart, onto the prepared cookie sheets, until you have 30 meringues. Flatten slightly.

5 Bake in a preheated oven for one hour, or until they peel off the baking parchment. Leave to cool. Whisk the vanilla sugar into the cream until thick.

6 Spread some cream on the flat side of a meringue, put some strawberries on top, spread some cream on another meringue, and sandwich together.

airtight container for up to 2 days

Baking

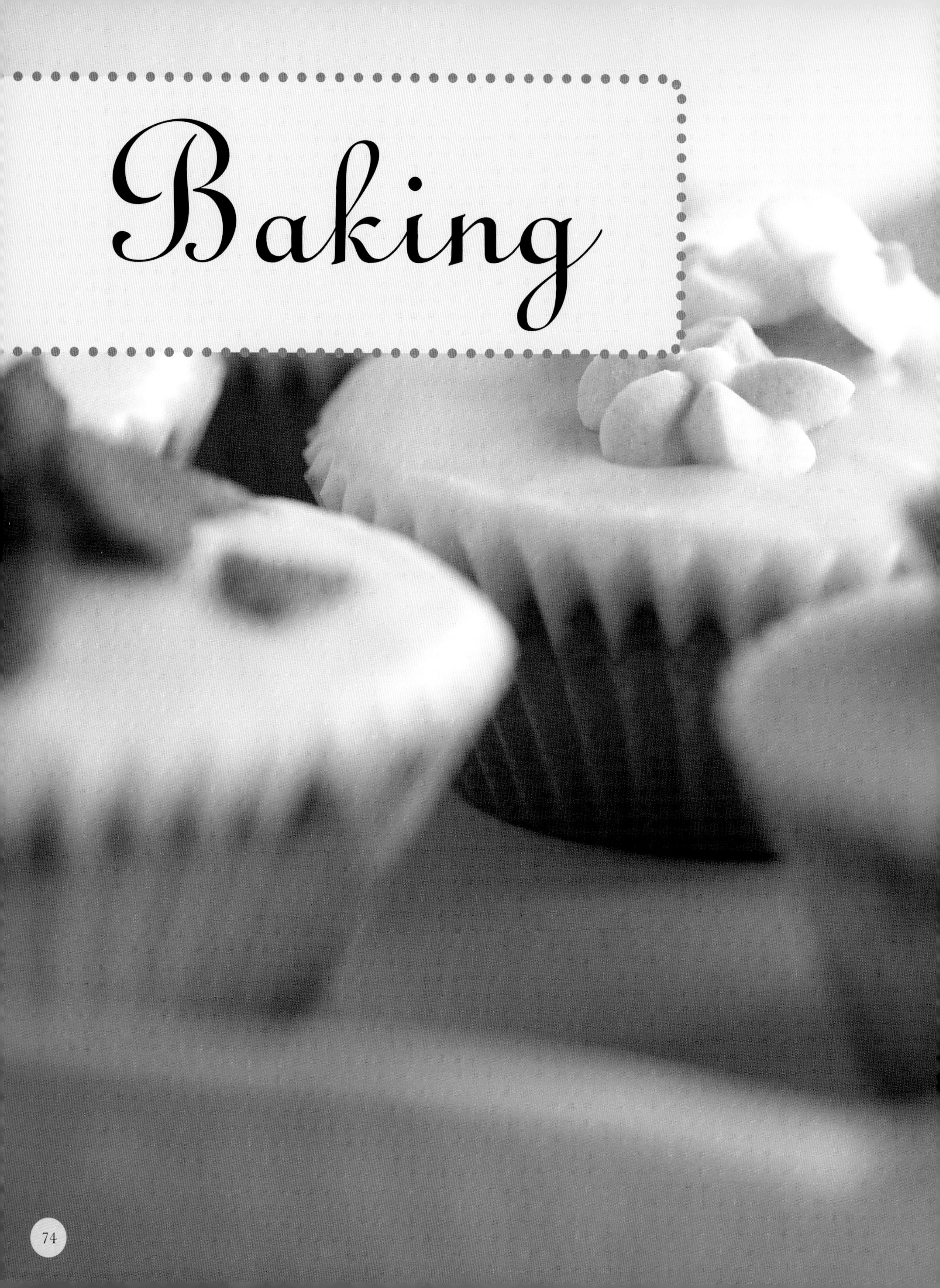

Makes 25 Preparation 3h Cooking 25

Fondant fancies

These gorgeous mini cakes take a while to prepare but are well worth the effort.

You can be really creative when

Ingredients

Cake:
- 7 oz (200 g) unsalted butter or margarine, softened
- 1 cup (200 g) sugar
- grated zest 1 lemon
- 4 medium eggs, beaten
- $1\frac{2}{3}$ cups (200 g) self-rising flour

Filling and icing:
- 3 oz (75 g) unsalted butter, softened
- $1\frac{3}{4}$ cup (175 g) confectioners' sugar, sifted
- 6 to 8 tbsp (90 to 120 ml) water
- 1 tbsp (15 ml) milk
- 1 tbsp (15 ml) apricot jam
- 4 oz (100 g) marzipan
- 2 lb (1 kg) bag fondant icing sugar
- 2 to 3 drops pink food coloring

Tools

- 2 bowls
- 2 spoons
- 8 in (20 cm) square pan
- baking parchment
- electric whisk
- palette knife
- bread knife
- plastic wrap
- rolling pin
- fork

1 Preheat the oven to 350°F (180°C). Grease and line the cake pan. Cream together the butter, sugar, and lemon zest.

2 Whisk in the eggs a little at a time, adding a little flour to prevent the mixture from curdling. Fold in remaining flour. Spoon into the pan; smooth the top.

3 Bake for 20 to 25 minutes. Cool in the pan. Turn out and with a bread knife remove the top layer of the cake, to make it even, then cut the cake in half horizontally.

4 Cream together the butter and confectioners' sugar; add the milk, and spread over one half of the cake. Sandwich together. Wrap in plastic wrap and chill for 2 hours.

5 Warm the apricot jam and spread over the top. Roll out the marzipan to an 8 in (20 cm) square and place on top of the cake. Cut the cake into 25 cubes.

6 Mix the fondant icing sugar and water until smooth. Add the coloring. Holding over the bowl, drizzle over each cube and decorate as desired. Leave to set.

you come to decorate these cakes!

Makes 24 Preparation 40 Cooking 32

Caramel shortbread

Caramel shortbread is also known as millionaires' shortbread. It is more like a cookie than a cake and is definitely for those with a sweet tooth!

Ingredients

Base:
- $\frac{1}{3}$ cup (50 g) soft brown sugar
- 4 oz (125 g) butter, softened
- $1\frac{1}{4}$ cups (150 g) self-rising flour

Caramel topping:
- 14 oz (400 g) can sweetened condensed milk
- 4 oz (125 g) butter, diced
- $\frac{1}{2}$ cup (75 g) soft light brown sugar
- 2 tbsp (50 ml) dark corn syrup

Chocolate topping:
- 3 oz (75 g) white chocolate
- 3 oz (75 g) dark chocolate

Tools

- 7 x 11 in (8 x 28 cm) baking pan
- baking parchment
- electric whisk
- mixing bowl
- wooden spoon
- saucepan
- 2 bowls
- metal spoon

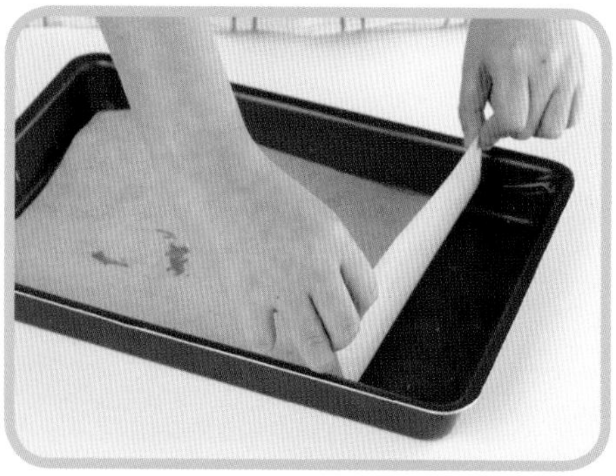

1 Preheat the oven to 350°F (180°C). Grease and line a 7 x 11 in (18 x 28 cm) pan with baking parchment.

2 Cream together the butter and sugar until light and fluffy. Stir in the flour and mix until combined.

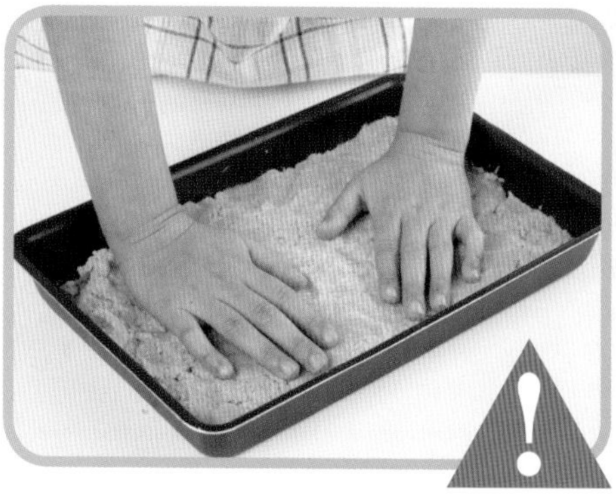

3 Press the mixture over the base of the pan and bake for 15 to 20 minutes until golden brown. Leave to cool.

These shortbread bites are lots of fun

4 Place the caramel topping ingredients in a saucepan. Place over a low heat until dissolved and bring to the boil. Continue to boil, stirring continuously, for 10 to 12 minutes.

5 Pour the caramel topping over the base. Leave to cool completely. Melt the chocolate in separate bowls over a pan of simmering water.

6 Pour the dark and white chocolate over the caramel and swirl together with the back of a spoon. Leave to set, then cut into squares.

to make. What patterns can you create?

Makes 12 Preparation 10 Cooking 20

Banocolate cookies

These banana-flavored cookies are combined with chunks of chocolate. They are best eaten on the day they are made, but can be stored in an airtight container for up to 2 days.

Try using different types of chocolate

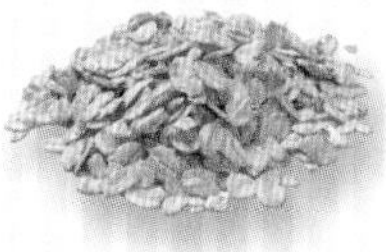

Ingredients

- 1 large ripe banana
- 4 oz (100 g) unsalted butter, cut into pieces
- 2/3 cup (100 g) soft light brown sugar
- 1 medium egg, beaten
- 1 cup (100 g) all-purpose flour
- 1/2 tsp (2.5 ml) baking powder
- 1/3 cup (50 g) oats
- 4 oz (100 g) dark chocolate, broken into small chunks

Tools

- 2 cookie sheets
- knife
- food processor
- mixing bowl
- metal spoon
- cooling rack

2 Preheat the oven to 350°F (180°C) and grease 2 cookie sheets with butter. Peel and slice the banana, then place in a food processor.

3 Add the butter, sugar, and egg and process until smooth. Add the flour, baking powder, and oats and pulse until combined.

4 Transfer the mixture to a bowl and stir in the chocolate chunks.

5 Drop heaped spoonfuls of the mixture onto the sheets. Flatten them then bake for 15 to 20 minutes. Cool for 5 minutes, then transfer to a cooling rack.

Top tip!

If you don't like banana, leave it out and add 2 tbsp (30 ml) of cocoa powder instead.

such as milk, white, dark, or flavored

Serves 10 Preparation 1.5h Cooking 12

Gingerbread house

For an extra surprise, fill the center of the house with more candies before attaching the roof.

Try making gingerbread men, women,

Ingredients

Dough:
- 9 oz (250 g) unsalted butter, softened
- 1 cup (150 g) soft brown sugar
- 2 medium eggs, beaten
- 6 fl oz (175 ml) dark corn syrup
- 2 tbsp (30 ml) ground ginger
- 5 cups (625 g) all-purpose flour
- 2 tsp (10 ml) baking soda

For decoration:
- 1 egg white
- 2 cups (225 g) confectioners' sugar
- marshmallows, halved, for the roof, and candies of your choice

Tools

- two 7 in x 4 in (18 cm x 10 cm) rectangles for the roof
- two 6 in x 4 in (15 cm x 10 cm) rectangles for the sides. Add windows
- two 4 in (10 cm) squares for the ends, extending 3 in ($7\frac{1}{2}$ cm) from the top of the squares to a point. Add a door
- food processor
- plastic wrap
- rolling pin
- baking parchment
- knife
- mixing bowl
- spoon
- cooling rack

1 Place the butter and sugar in a food processor and blend until creamy. Add the eggs, corn syrup, ginger, baking soda, and half the flour and process.

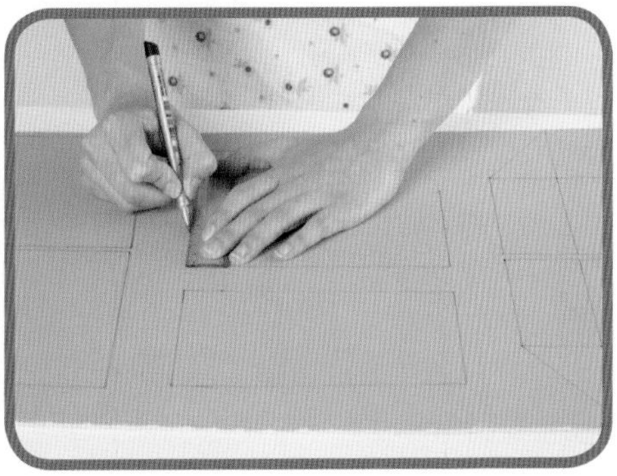

2 Add the remaining flour and process until the mixture forms a ball. Wrap in plastic wrap and chill for 30 minutes. Meanwhile, cut out the templates.

3 Preheat the oven to 350°F (180°C). Roll out the dough between 2 pieces of baking parchment to $\frac{1}{4}$ in (5 mm) thick. Use the templates to cut the dough.

4 Chill for 10 minutes, then bake for 12 minutes. Leave to cool for 2 minutes, then transfer to a cooling rack. Beat the egg white and confectioners' sugar together.

5 Join the front and sides of the house together with a little of the icing and allow to dry. Add the back and roof in the same way. Decorate with icing and candy.

and children to live in your house

Serves 10 Preparation 15 Cooking 30

Chocolate cake

This moist cake is simple to make. Decorate as desired with candies, chocolate curls, or sprinkles.

This yummy cake is perfect for

Ingredients

- 1 cup (200 g) sugar
- 7 oz (200g) butter, softened
- 4 medium eggs, beaten
- 1⅔ cups (200 g) self-rising flour. Swap 3 tbsp (45ml) for 3 tbsp (45 ml) cocoa powder
- 1 tsp (5 ml) baking powder
- 2 tbsp (30 ml) milk

Ganache:

- 10 fl oz (284 ml) carton heavy cream
- 2 tbsp (30 ml) sugar
- 7 oz (200 g) good quality dark chocolate, broken into pieces

Tools

- 2 x 8 in (20 cm) round cake pans
- baking parchment
- large mixing bowl
- electric whisk
- spatula
- cooling rack
- saucepan
- wooden spoon
- bowl
- palette knife

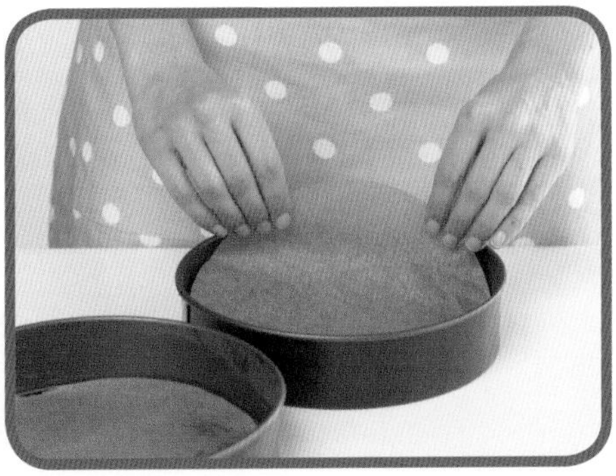

1 Preheat oven to 375°F (190°C). Butter two 8 in (20 cm) round cake pans and line with nonstick baking parchment.

2 In a large bowl, whisk all the cake ingredients together until you have a smooth, soft batter.

3 Divide the mixture between the pans, smooth the surface with a spatula, then bake for about 20 minutes. Turn onto a cooling rack and leave to cool.

4 Place the cream and sugar in a pan and heat until it is about to boil. Put the chocolate in a bowl and pour the cream over. Stir until the chocolate melts.

5 Sandwich the cake together with a little of the ganache. Pour the rest over the top and sides of the cake and smooth with a palette knife. Decorate as desired.

Top tip!

This cake can also be served warm—heat in a microwave and serve with a scoop of ice cream.

Makes 48 Preparation 10 Cooking 12

Mini muffins

These bite-sized treats are bursting with fruitiness. You will need to cook them in two batches.

These scrumptious muffins are

Ingredients

- 2¼ cups (280 g) flour
- 1 tbsp (15 ml) baking powder
- ½ tsp (2.5 ml) salt
- ⅔ cup (125 g) sugar
- 1 large egg
- 2 bananas, roughly chopped
- 8 fl oz (240 ml) milk
- 3 oz (85 g) melted butter
- 1⅓ cups (200 g) blueberries

Tools

- 2 x 12 mini muffin pans
- strainer
- 2 mixing bowls
- fork
- measuring cup
- metal spoon
- whisk

1 Preheat the oven to 400°F (200°C). Line 2 x 12 mini muffin pans with paper cases.

2 In a large bowl, sift together flour, baking powder, and salt. Stir in the sugar.

3 In a small bowl, mash the bananas with a fork.

4 In a measuring cup, whisk together the egg, milk, and butter, then add to the mashed banana, stirring to combine.

5 Add all the wet ingredients to the dry. Stir to just combine, then fold in the blueberries.

6 Spoon into the cases and bake for 10 to 12 minutes or until lightly browned. Refill the muffin pans with paper cases and repeat with the remaining mixture.

a perfect afternoon snack!

Makes 20 Preparation 30 Cooking 15

Cupcakes

Cook these pretty cupcakes and decorate with pastel colored icings, candies, or crystalized flowers. Stack in a tower as an alternative way to celebrate a birthday party or get-together.

Top tip!

These cupcakes can be made the day before and stored in an airtight container.

These cupcakes are easy and quick to

Ingredients

Cakes:
- 6 oz (150 g) unsalted butter, softened
- $\frac{3}{4}$ cup (150 g) sugar
- $1\frac{1}{4}$ cups (150 g) self-rising flour
- 3 medium eggs, whisked
- $\frac{1}{2}$ tsp (2.5 ml) vanilla extract

Icing and decoration:
- 2 cups (225 g) confectioners' sugar
- 2 to 3 tbsp (30 to 45 ml) hot water
- 3 different food colorings
- Edible crystalized flowers, sugar strands, sprinkles, or candies

Tools

- 2 muffin pans
- 20 paper cases
- 2 mixing bowls
- wooden spoon
- 2 metal spoons
- cooling rack
- knife
- 3 small mixing bowls

1 Line 2 x 12 muffin pans with 20 paper cases. Preheat the oven to 350°F (180°C).

2 Place the butter, sugar, self-rising flour, eggs, and vanilla extract in a bowl and beat with a wooden spoon until pale and creamy.

3 Divide between the paper cases. Bake for 15 minutes until golden and just firm. Cool in the pan for 5 minutes, then transfer to a cooling rack to cool.

4 Trim any pointed tops to make a flat surface.

5 Place the icing in a large bowl, gradually beat in sufficient water to give a smooth, thick icing that coats the back of a spoon.

6 Transfer the icing mixture to 3 individual bowls and add a few drops of food coloring to each. Spoon onto the cupcakes and top with decorations. Allow to set.

make, and even quicker to eat!

Makes 16 Preparation 15 Cooking 40

Chocolate & raspberry brownies

These delicious pretty brownies, dotted with fresh raspberries and white chocolate, are so easy to make.

These yummy white chocolate and raspberry

Ingredients

- 9 oz (250 g) good quality white chocolate
- 3 oz (75 g) butter
- $\frac{2}{3}$ cup (125 g) sugar
- 2 large eggs, beaten
- 1 tsp (5 ml) vanilla extract
- $1\frac{1}{4}$ cups (150 g) flour
- $\frac{1}{2}$ tsp (2.5 ml) salt
- 1 cup (150 g) fresh raspberries

Tools

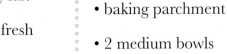

- 8 in (20 cm) square cake pan
- baking parchment
- 2 medium bowls
- saucepan
- electric whisk
- strainer
- metal spoon
- plastic spatula
- knife

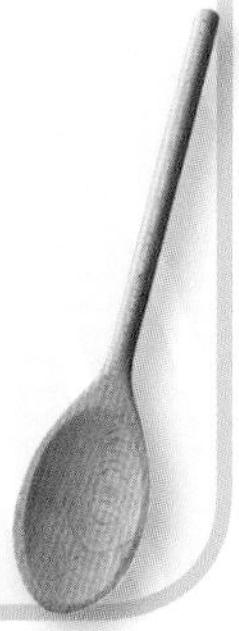

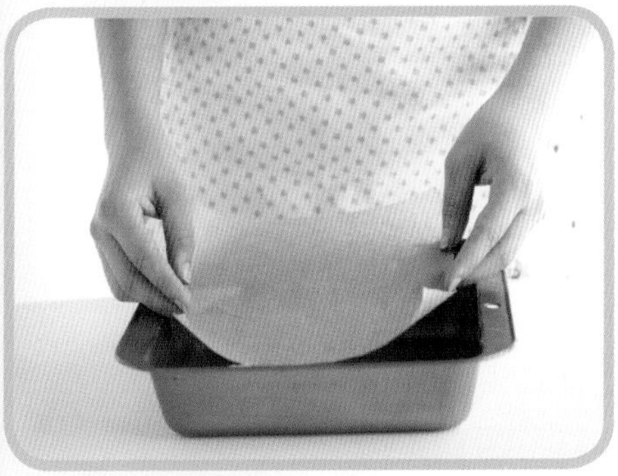

1 Preheat the oven to 350°F (180°C). Grease and line the bottom of an 8 in (20 cm) square cake pan with baking parchment.

2 Break up the chocolate and put 6 oz (175 g) in a bowl and set over a pan of simmering water until melted and smooth. Cool slightly.

3 Whisk the butter and sugar together until fluffy in a medium bowl. Whisk in the eggs and vanilla extract, then stir in the melted chocolate.

4 Sift the flour and salt over the mixture and fold in. Then gently fold in the saved broken chocolate and the raspberries.

5 Spoon the mixture into the pan, spread into the corners, and level with a plastic spatula. Cook for 30 to 35 minutes. Cool before cutting into squares.

Top tip!

Brownies should be firm on the outside but gooey and fudgelike on the inside.

brownies are a perfect snack!

Drinks

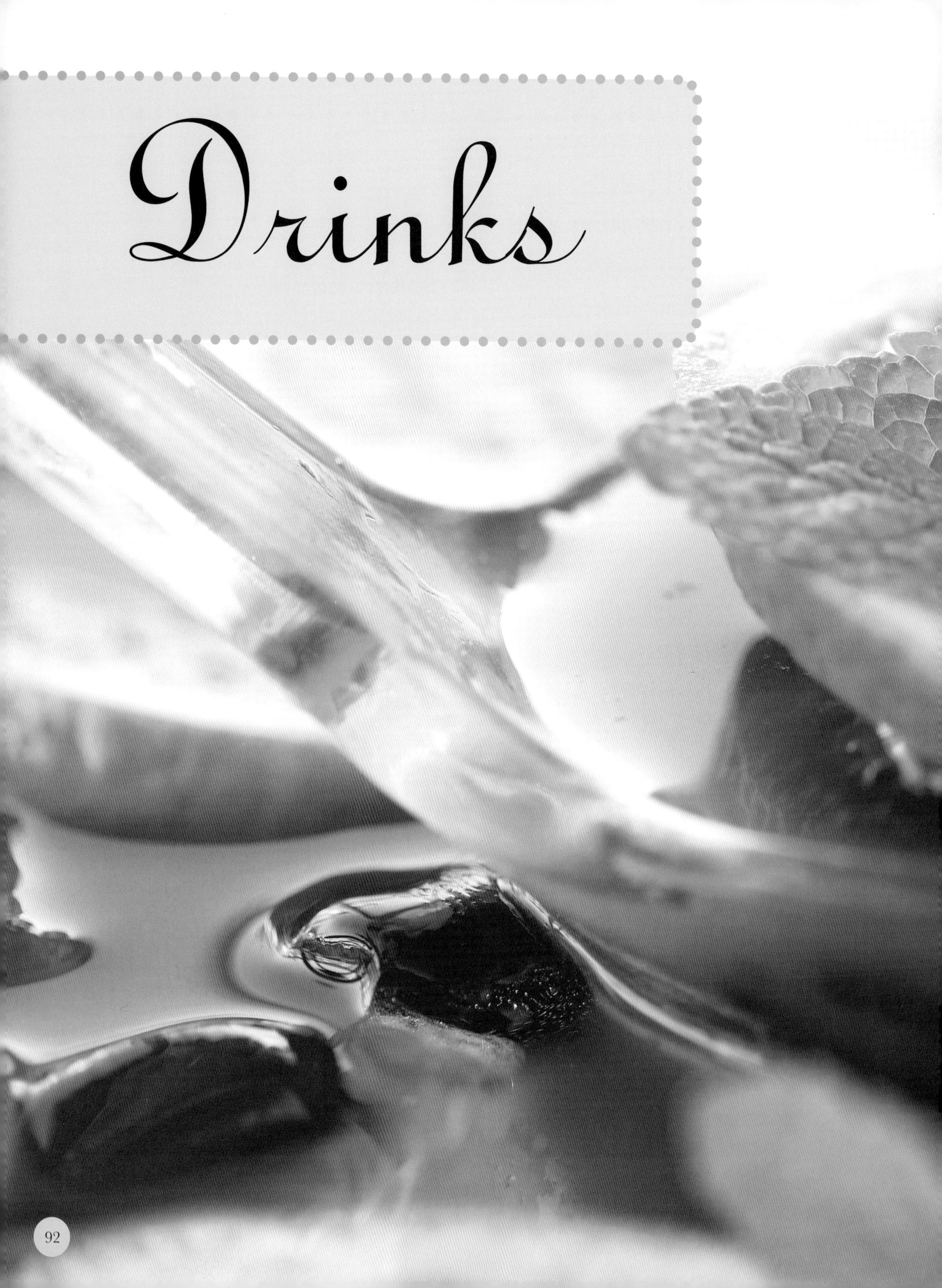

Serves 4 Preparation 5

Milkshake

Make your own delicious milkshakes with fresh fruit. This simple drink is healthy and full of natural goodness.

Ingredients

- 1 lb (400 g) fresh strawberries or 4 bananas
- 2 cups (600 ml) cold milk
- 8 scoops vanilla ice cream

Tools

- knife
- cutting board
- blender

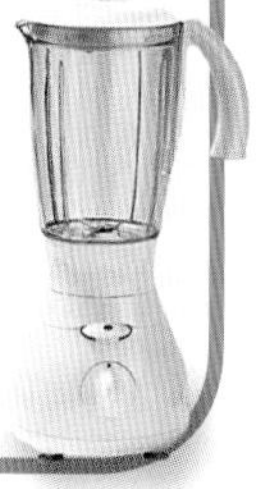

1 Remove the stalks from the strawberries/peel and chop the banana. Place in a liquidizer or blender and blitz to a purée.

2 Add the milk and ice cream and blend for 1 minute until frothy. Pour into 4 tall glasses and serve. For the banana one, try adding 4 tbsp of toffee sauce or try chocolate ice cream instead of vanilla.

Decorate your glass with extra fruit

Serves 4 Preparation 5 Cooking 4

Hot chocolate

This simple recipe uses good quality chocolate instead of powdered chocolate—the taste is so much better!

Ingredients

- 4 oz (100 g) good quality dark, milk, or white chocolate
- $2\frac{1}{2}$ cups (600 ml) milk
- few drops of mint, orange, or vanilla extract
- 12 marshmallows
- cocoa powder, for dusting

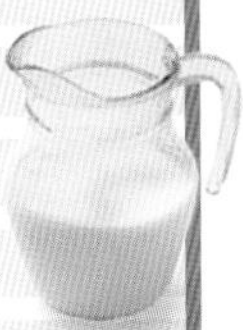

Tools

- grater
- whisk
- saucepan

1 Coarsely grate the chocolate. Place the milk and chocolate in a saucepan and whisk over a moderate heat for 3 to 4 minutes until the chocolate has dissolved.

2 Add a few drops of flavoring. Pour the hot chocolate into 4 mugs and top each with 3 marshmallows. Dust with the cocoa powder.

Deliciously flavored hot chocolate!

Cherry cordial

Make this cordial when cherries are in season. Top with chilled sparkling water and ice for a refreshing drink.

This cherry cordial is a refreshing

Ingredients

- 2 lb (1 kg) fresh red cherries
- $2\frac{1}{2}$ cups (600 ml) cold water
- $1\frac{3}{4}$ cups (350 g) sugar
- chilled still or sparkling water and ice, to serve

Tools

- knife
- cutting board
- 2 large saucepans
- wooden spoon
- food processor
- strainer
- metal spoon
- sterile jars

1 Cut each cherry in half and remove the pit. Place the pitted cherries in a medium pan with the cold water.

2 Bring to the boil and simmer over a gentle heat for about 15 minutes until the fruit has softened.

3 Leave to cool for 10 minutes, then place in a food processor and blend. (You may need to do this in batches.)

4 Mash through a strainer into a clean pan, pressing the pulp left in the strainer. Add the sugar and, over a low heat, stir until dissolved.

5 Simmer for 5 minutes. Pour into sterilized jars and store in a cool place. Pour a little of the cordial into a glass and top with chilled water and ice.

Top tip!

To make a black currant cordial replace the cherries with the same weight of black currants.

drink for a hot summer's day!

Watermelon punch

This pretty red punch is made from watermelon and raspberries.

Ingredients

- 1 small watermelon
- $2\frac{1}{2}$ cups (300 g) fresh raspberries
- 1 orange, sliced
- 20 fresh mint leaves
- 20 ice cubes
- extra raspberries, to serve

Tools

- knife
- cutting board
- blender
- large bowl
- stainer

1 Cut the watermelon in half, then cut into wedges, and remove the skin. Cut the flesh into chunks—you need about 2 lb (1 kg). Place in a blender with the raspberries and blend until liquified.

2 Strain the mixture through a strainer over a bowl. Pour into a cup or punch bowl and add the orange slices, mint, and ice cubes. Add the extra raspberries. Serve immediately.

This delicious drink is full of goodness

Smoothies

Fruit smoothies not only make a nutritional drink, but can also be served as a healthy snack, or with cereal or toast for breakfast.

Ingredients

- 3 cups (12 oz or 350 g) mixed berries
- 1 ripe banana
- 16 oz (500 g) low-fat or fat-free vanilla bio live yogurt
- 1 cup (300 ml) low-fat milk

Tools

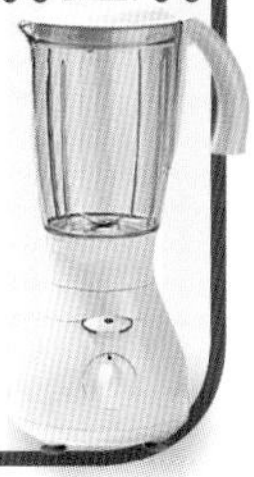

- knife
- blender

1 Peel the banana and roughly break into small pieces. Place in a blender with the berries, yogurt, and milk. Whizz until the mixture is thick and smooth.

2 Pour into glasses and serve at once. For a banana and mango smoothie, substitute the berries for 1 large ripe mango and add another banana.

Choose which flavor you like best!

Serves 5 Preparation 15

Pink lemonade

There is nothing more refreshing than a cool glass of homemade lemonade. Pink lemonade was traditionally dyed with a little beet juice, but this recipe uses cranberry juice for flavor and color.

Ingredients

- 4 unwaxed lemons
- ½ cup (100 g) sugar
- 2½ cups (600 ml) boiling water
- ¾ cup (200 ml) cranberry juice, chilled
- ¾ cup (200 ml) water, chilled
- ice and lemon slices

Tools

- potato peeler
- knife
- cutting board
- wooden spoon
- measuring cup
- mini-strainer
- serving pitcher

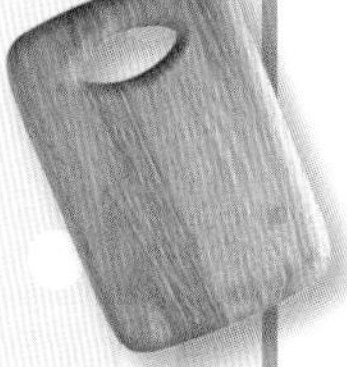

1 Using a potato peeler, peel the zest from the lemons, leaving as much of the white pith on the lemons as possible. Squeeze the juice from the lemons.

2 Pour the lemon juice into a large heatproof measuring cup, add the sugar and lemon zest. Pour over the boiling water and stir until the sugar has dissolved.

3 Leave to cool. Then strain the lemonade into a serving pitcher.

4 Stir in the cranberry juice and chilled water. Sweeten with extra sugar if desired and serve in glasses with ice and a slice of lemon.

This decorative drink is

Very pretty and tastes great!

Sweets & treats

Makes 24 Preparation 10 Cooking 5

Marshmallow squares

These delicious squares of marshmallow and toasted rice cereal are so easy to make and will keep in an airtight container for up to a week.

Ingredients

- 5 cups (250 g) miniature marshmallows
- $^{1}/_{2}$ tsp (2.5 ml) vanilla
- 4 oz (100 g) butter, diced
- 6 cups (175 g) toasted rice cereal

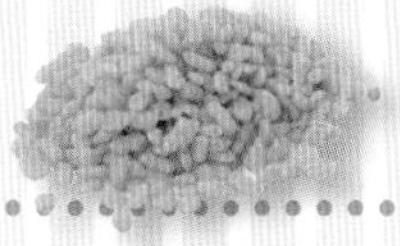

Tools

- 7 x 11 in (18 x 28 cm) oblong pan
- saucepan
- wooden spoon
- metal spoon
- knife

1 Grease a 7 x 11 in (18 x 28 cm) oblong pan. Place $^{3}/_{4}$ of the marshmallows, with the butter and vanilla extract, in a medium saucepan.

2 Place over a medium heat and cook until the butter and marshmallows have melted. Roughly chop the remaining marshmallows.

3 Mix the toasted rice cereal with the marshmallow mixture, then stir in the extra marshmallows. Spoon the mixture into the pan; press down with the back of a spoon.

4 Allow to cool in the pan and then cut into squares.

These are perfect to make if you don't have

Top tip!

Use different colored marshmallows to make your squares look more colorful.

much time since they are so quick & easy!

Serves 6 Preparation 5 Cooking 5

Toffee popcorn

Homemade popcorn is lots of fun to make and tastes much better than store-bought.

Top tip!
If you prefer salted popcorn, just leave out the toffee sauce and sprinkle over some salt.

Ingredients

- 2 tbsp (30 ml) corn oil
- $3\frac{1}{2}$ oz (100 g) unpopped popcorn
- 3 tbsp (75 ml) corn syrup
- $\frac{1}{3}$ cup (50 g) brown sugar
- 2 oz (50 g) butter

Tools

- 2 medium saucepans
- large mixing bowl
- spoon

1 Heat the oil in a saucepan. Add the popcorn and, with the lid on, shake to coat in the oil. Over a medium heat, shake the pan occasionally until the corn has popped.

2 Remove from the heat. Place the butter, sugar, and syrup in another pan. Stir together over a medium heat until the butter has melted and the sugar has dissolved.

3 Put the popcorn into a large mixing bowl and drizzle the toffee sauce over the top.

4 Stir until the popcorn is coated. Stop stirring when the sauce has cooled and is setting. Leave until cool enough to eat.

This recipe makes the perfect

Top tip!

Wait until there is 3 to 5 seconds between each "pop" before you turn off the heat.

accompaniment to your favorite movies!

Makes 60 Preparation 20

Peppermint creams

These sophisticated candies make a gorgeous gift for a friend—or maybe for yourself!

Ingredients

- $4^1/_2$ cups (450 g) confectioners' sugar, sifted
- 8 to 9 tbsp (120 to 135 ml) sweetened condensed milk
- few drops peppermint extract or essence
- few drops green food coloring
- 6 oz (150 g) dark chocolate

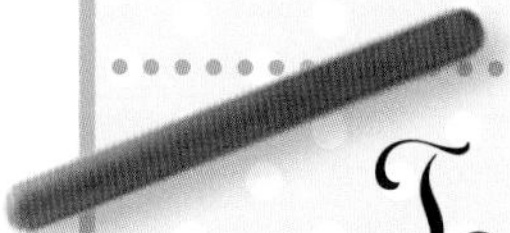

Tools

- mixing bowl
- metal spoon
- rolling pin
- small circular cookie cutter
- baking parchment
- heatproof bowl
- saucepan

1 Place the confectioners' sugar in a large bowl and add the condensed milk. Stir until you have a crumbly mixture.

2 Add a few drops of the peppermint extract or essence, and a few drops of green food coloring. Knead until you have a smooth firm mixture.

3 Dust the work surface with a little confectioners' sugar and roll out to $^1/_2$ in (5 mm) thick. Cut into rounds with a small cutter. Leave to dry on baking parchment.

4 Melt the chocolate in a heatproof bowl over a pan of simmering water, then dip each cream into the melted chocolate. Leave to set.

The combination of chocolate

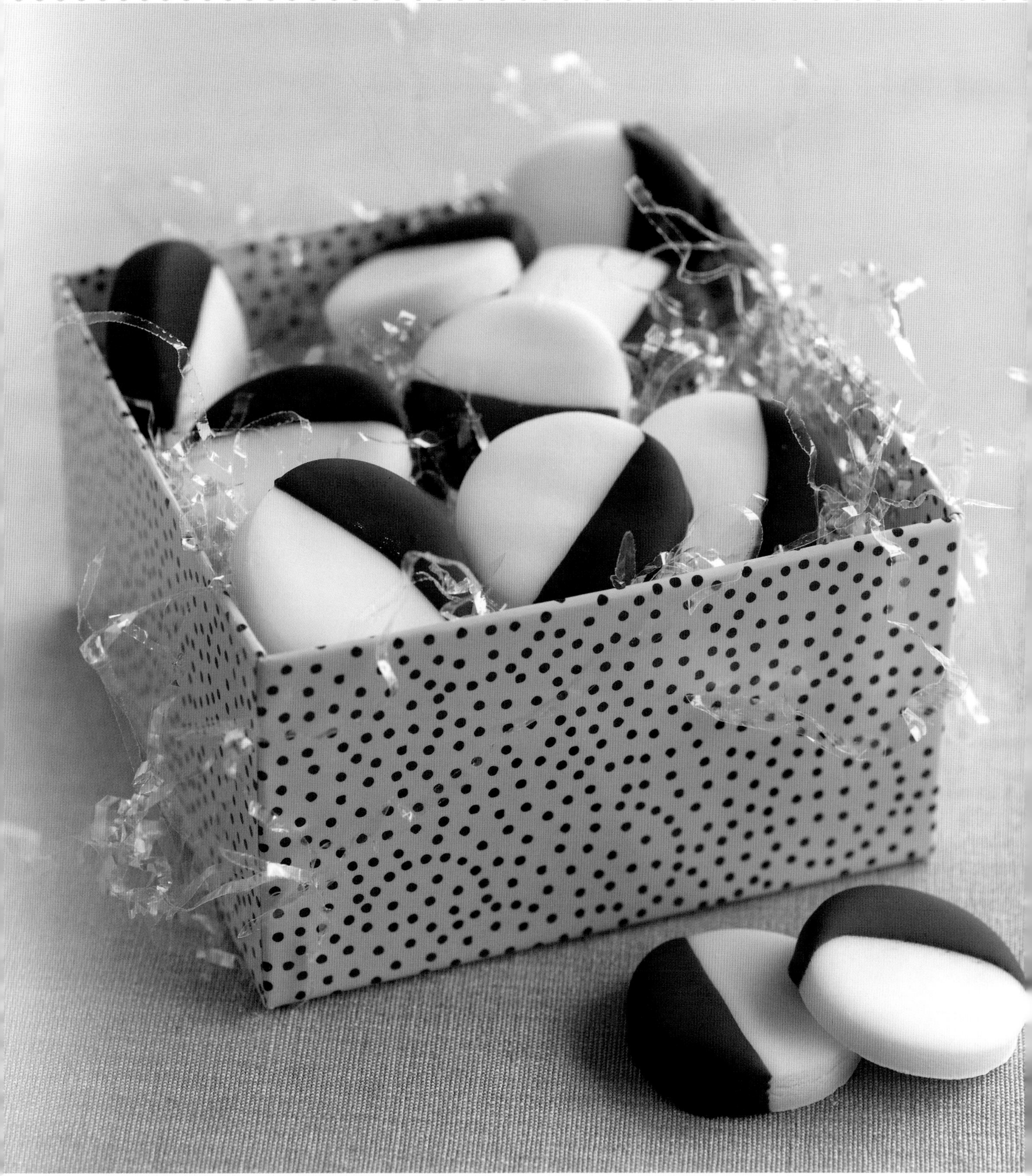

and mint flavors is scrumptious!

Makes 36 Preparation 5 Cooking 30

Ultimate fudge

Homemade candies make wonderful gifts or treats. This basic recipe can be adapted to make chocolate or raisin fudge.

Top tip!
As with all sweets and treats, eat fudge in moderation or you will feel sick!

Ingredients

- $2^1/_4$ cups (450 g) sugar
- 2 oz (50 g) unsalted butter, diced
- 6 fl oz (170 g) can evaporated milk
- $^3/_4$ cup (150 ml) milk
- $^1/_2$ tsp (2.5 ml) vanilla extract

Tools

- 7 in (18 cm) shallow nonstick square pan
- medium heavy-based saucepan
- candy thermometer
- wooden spoon
- knife

1 Grease a 7 in (18 cm) shallow nonstick square pan.

2 Gently heat the sugar, butter, and milks in a saucepan, stirring with a wooden spoon until all the sugar has dissolved.

3 Bring to the boil and simmer gently, stirring continuously, for about 20 to 25 minutes.

Give fudge as a gift, beautifully

4 A candy thermometer should reach a temperature of 240°F (116°C). Remove from the heat, and add the vanilla extract.

5 Beat until the mixture is thick and paler in color. Pour into the prepared pan and leave to cool. When cold, cut into squares.

Top tip!

For chocolate fudge stir in 6 oz (150 g) melted dark chocolate in place of the vanilla. For raisin fudge, stir in 3 oz (75 g) chopped raisins.

presented in a homemade giftbox (p. 117)

Makes 20 Preparation 2.5h Cooking 5

Chocolate truffles

You can flavor these truffles with vanilla, orange, or peppermint extract and roll them in cocoa powder, chocolate sprinkles, or chopped nuts.

Ingredients

- 8 oz (200 g) milk chocolate
- 4 fl oz (100 ml) heavy cream
- ½ oz (15 g) unsalted butter
- few drops of orange, vanilla, or peppermint extract (optional)

To decorate:

- sifted cocoa powder
- grated milk, dark, and white chocolate
- chopped nuts, e.g., pistachios

Tools

- medium-sized bowl
- small saucepan
- wooden spoon
- plate

1 Break the chocolate into small pieces in a medium sized bowl. Put the cream in a small saucepan with the butter and bring slowly to the boil.

2 Immediately pour over the broken chocolate. With a wooden spoon, stir until the mixture is smooth and all the chocolate has melted.

3 Stir in a few drops of orange or peppermint extract if using. Cover and allow the mixture to cool for about 30 minutes at room temperature.

For a pure and simple hit of chocolate,

4 Chill in the refrigerator for about 2 hours. Using a teaspoon, scoop out bite-sized pieces. Dust your hand lightly with cocoa powder and roll into balls.

5 Immediately roll the truffles in sifted cocoa powder, grated chocolate, or nuts. Place in individual foil candy cases and chill. They will keep for up to 10 days.

Top tip!

Alternatively, you can dip the truffles in melted milk, dark, or white chocolate.

these truffles are just the thing!

Makes 72 Preparation 15

Coconut ice

This coconut ice recipe requires no cooking—just mix all the ingredients together and leave to set.

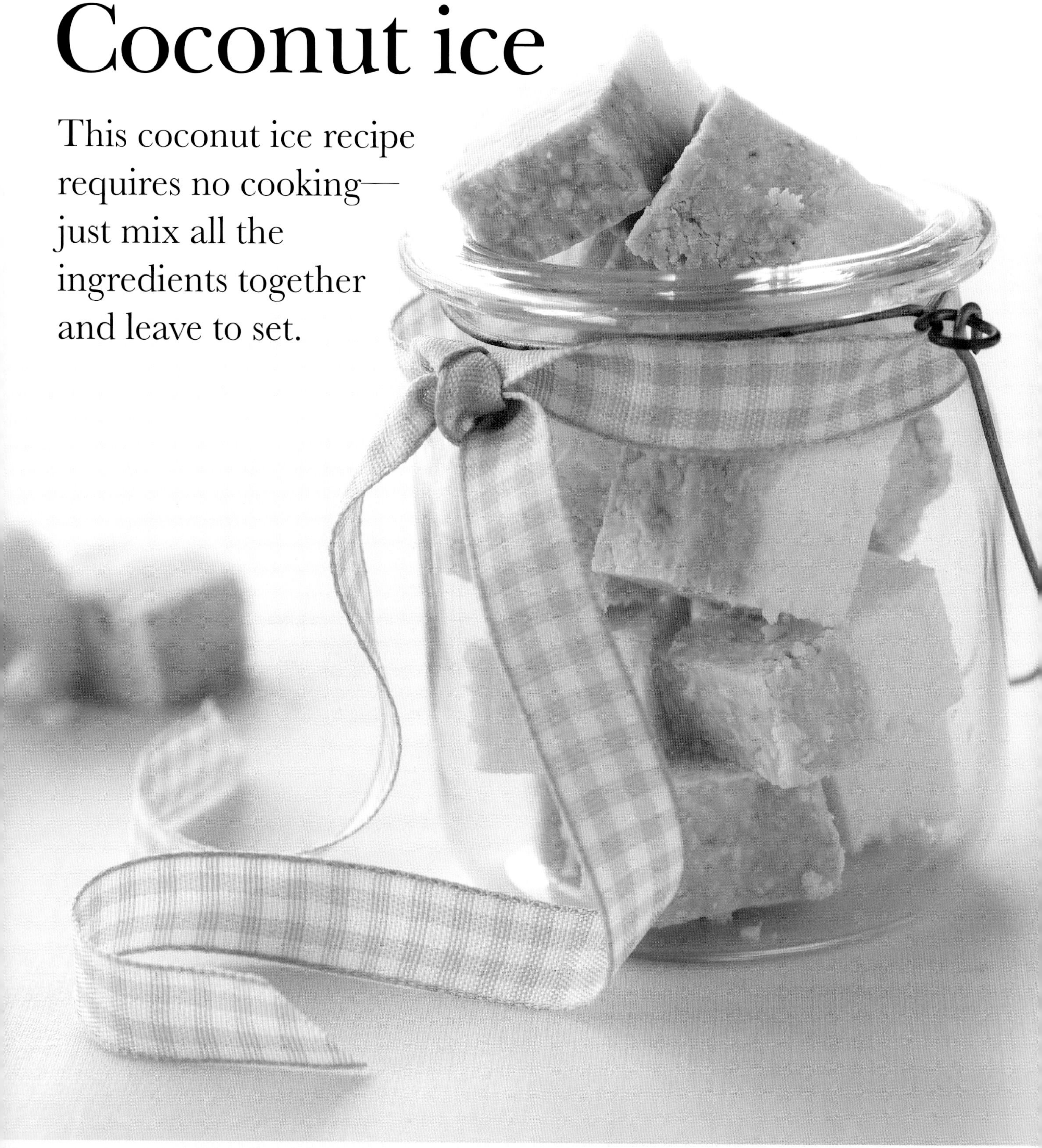

Try using different food colorings

Ingredients

- 14 oz (400 g) can sweetened condensed milk
- 5 cups (500 g) confectioners' sugar, sifted
- 4 cups (350 g) shredded coconut
- few drops pink food coloring

Tools

- 8 in (20 cm) square cake pan
- baking parchment
- mixing bowl
- metal spoon

1 Line an 8 in (20 cm) square cake pan with baking parchment.

2 In a large bowl, combine the condensed milk with the confectioners' sugar, then stir in the coconut, to form a stiff mixture.

Top tip!

If stored in an airtight container, the coconut ice will keep for up to 3 weeks.

3 Divide the mixture in half and using your hands, press half into the pan.

4 Knead the remaining mixture with a few drops of pink coloring and dusted with a little confectioners' sugar.

5 Press this over the white layer. Refrigerate until set, then cut into squares.

instead of the traditional pink and white

Crafts

Gift boxes

Make these beautiful gift boxes filled with scrumptious treats to give as gifts to friends or family.

You will need

- plain box
- paint
- paintbrush
- scissors
- a selection of colored paper
- double-sided tape
- glue
- ribbons
- glitter and gems
- tissue paper

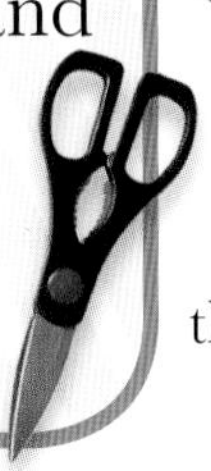

1 Paint the box, then cut out some flower shapes from the different papers and stick to the lid of the box.

2 Add some ribbon around the box and decorate with glitter and gems. Line with tissue paper.

Makes 1 Preparation 20

Invitations

Making your own party invitations will give your party a sense of occasion. Your friends will appreciate the extra effort you have put in to make your party a special event!

 Be sure to add lots of glitter and sparkle

You will need

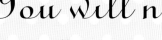

- 1 sheet $8^1/_2$ x 11 in white poster board
- 1 sheet 11 x 14 in pink poster board
- ruler
- pencil
- scissors
- various sheets of colored construction and glitter paper
- adhesive gems, sequins, and felt flowers
- glue
- ribbons

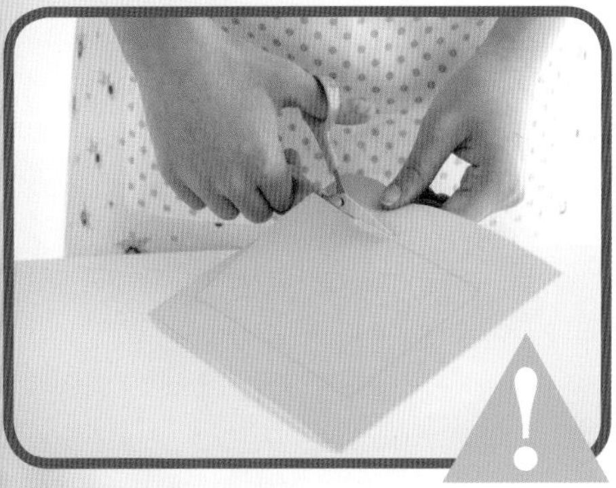

1 Fold the piece of white poster board in half to make the base. Draw a border of 1 in (2.5 cm) around the pink poster board and then cut out the middle.

2 Cut some balloon and present shapes out of different colored paper. Accessorize with glitter paper to look like ribbon and sparkly jewels.

Top tip!

Deliver your invitations to your friends and have a great time at your party!

3 Cut out a dress shape using poster board. Use glitter paper for the coat hanger. Fold fabric strips like an accordion and stick to double-sided tape for the ruffles.

4 Using gems, ribbon, and felt flowers, accessorize the border. Stick the border on to the white poster board. Glue presents, balloons, and dress inside the border.

5 Accessorize the envelope with ribbon, felt flowers, and gems. Remember to write the details of your party inside!

to make these cards truly extraordinary!

Makes 1 *Preparation* 15

Place settings

If you are planning a dinner party, why not make these gorgeous named place settings to show your guests where to sit.

If your dinner party has a theme you

You will need

- 2 different colored pieces of poster board
- pencil
- ruler
- scissors
- double-sided tape or craft glue
- thread
- needle
- adhesive tape
- gems and glitter beads
- glitter glue
- silver star decorations

1 Cut out a thick strip of poster board and divide into 3 equal sections, with a ½ in (1 cm) strip at one end. Score along all the lines.

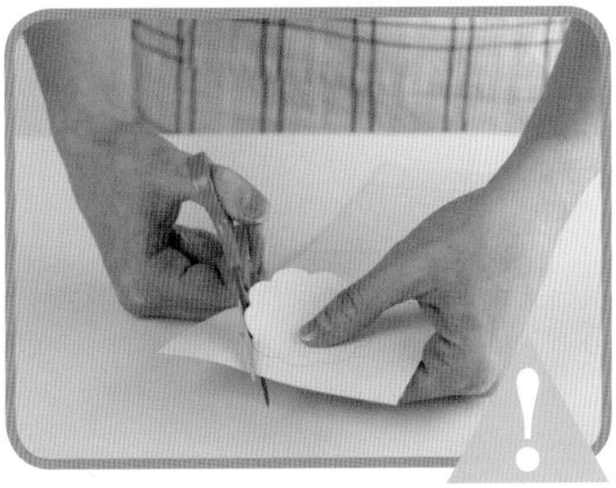

2 Draw and cut out a pretty shape in the first section.

3 Cover the back of your strip with colored paper so it's not white when you look through your shape.

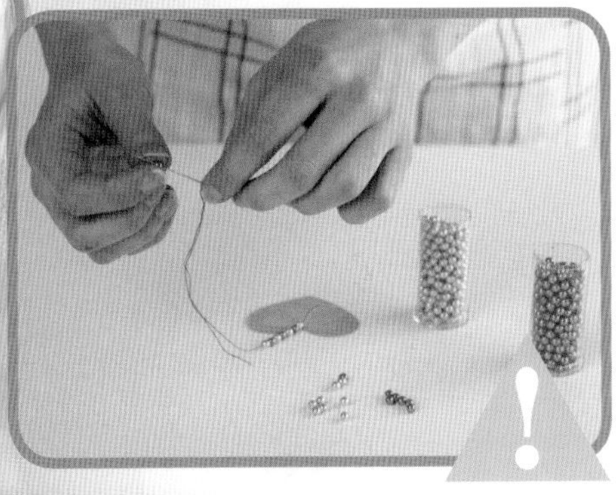

4 Cut a heart shape out of poster board. Stick some thread to the heart and thread some beads on using the needle.

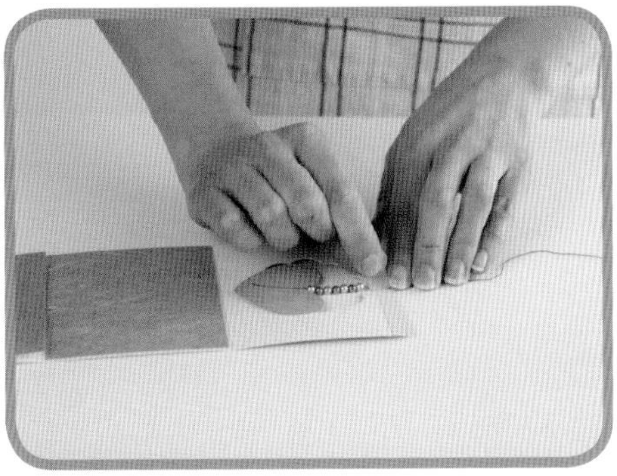

5 Tape the thread onto the back of the section with the pretty shape cut out of it. Trim the end of the thread neatly.

6 Using double-sided tape or glue, stick the ½ in (1 cm) strip to the back of the front section.

can adapt these place settings to match

Makes 3 Preparation 20

Drink mixers

These pretty mixers will add a touch of class to any beverage. Wash them carefully after use and use again and again.

Match the color of the drink mixers

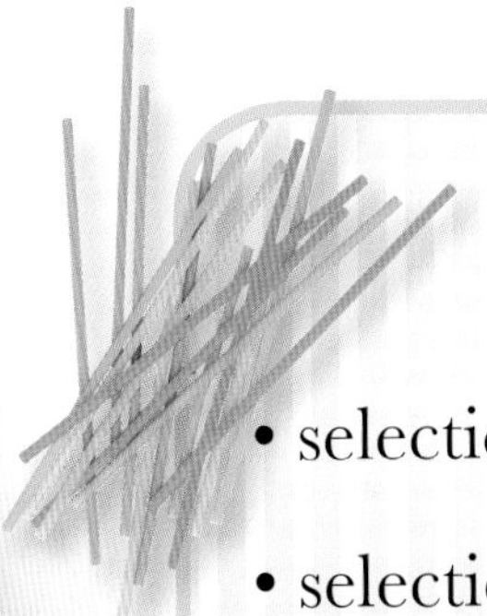

You will need

- selection of straws
- selection of papers, material, and poster board
- sequins and gems
- glue
- double-sided tape

Top tip!

If you don't like these shapes, try making a mixer in the shape of your favorite animal.

Star mixer

1 Cut out two star shapes and stick them on to the top of a straw.

2 Cut smaller star shapes out of different patterned material and construction paper and stick them on top to create a layered effect. Add star sequins to finish.

Flower mixer

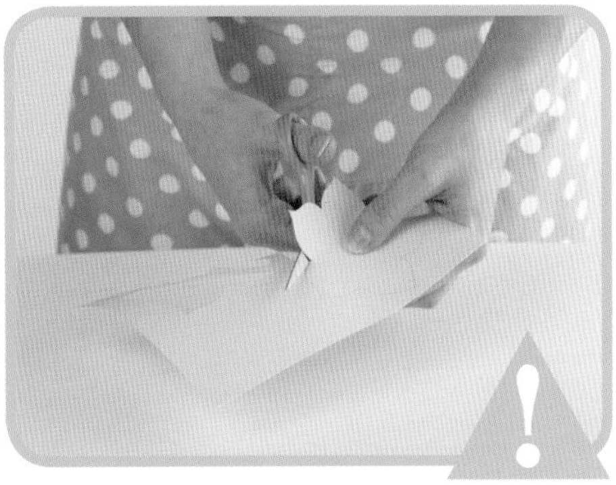

1 Cut a pretty flower shape out of poster board or construction paper.

2 Cut out some smaller, different flower shapes to stick on top. Make them different shapes. Add gems and glue to the straw.

Butterfly mixer

1 Cut out two butterfly shapes and bend the wings outward. Cut some pretty shapes out of colored paper or poster board and stick to the wings and body.

2 Stick the butterfly bodies to the top of the straw and decorate the edges of the wings with gems.

to your friends' favorite colors

Makes 1 Preparation 15

Folded napkins

These folded napkins are very easy and quick to make. Adding sequins, gems, and decorations will add some sparkle to a dinner party. Try experimenting with your favorite colors.

You will need

- lots of colored paper napkins
- glitter and gems
- craft glue

Top tip!

For an extra-special effect, color-coordinate these napkins with the place settings.

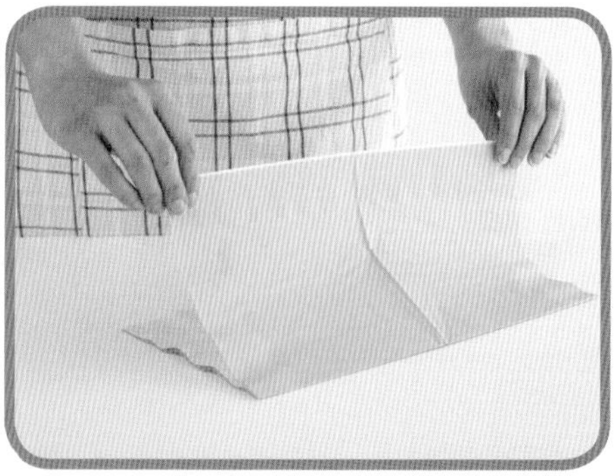

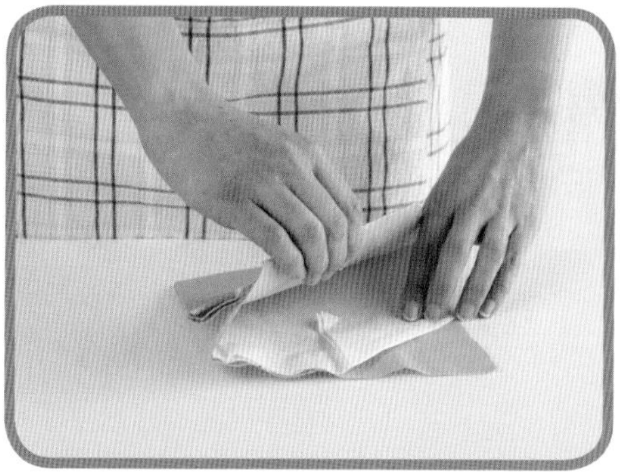

1 Place 2 different colored napkins together and fold them in half and then in half again.

2 Take the top loose corner of the first sheet and fold underneath to make a pocket.

3 Repeat with the other layers, leaving a 1/2 in (1 cm) strip between each fold.

These napkins will add an elegant

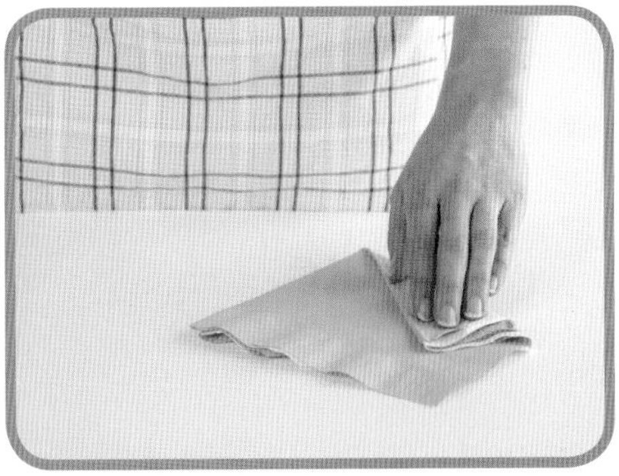

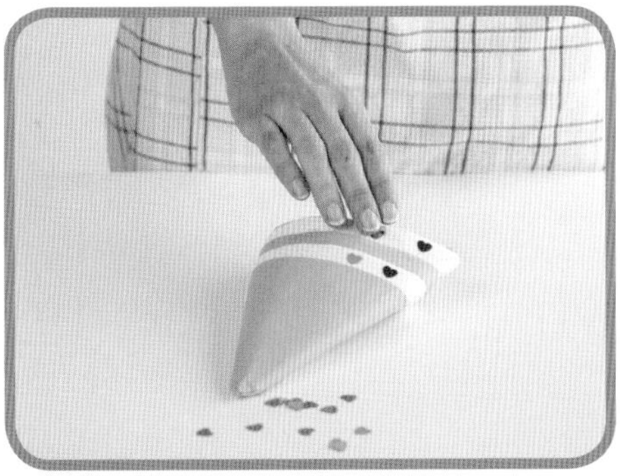

Top tip!

Try creating other folded napkin styles, such as these below.

4 Turn the napkins over and fold the two side corners into the center to create a cone shape.

5 Decorate with gems and sparkles. Open the pocket to place your knife and fork inside.

finishing touch to your table

Glossary

If you don't know what a word means, look it up here!

A

accompaniment a food dish that is served with the main dish. It is often made from vegetables or potato.

B

batch a quantity of things cooked together at the same time.
batter a mixture of flour, egg, and milk or water, used for coating food for frying.
beat to stir or mix an ingredient quickly, to add air.
béchamel a white sauce made from butter, milk, and flour.
blend to mix ingredients by hand or in a blender or food processor to form a liquid or smooth mixture.
brown to cook food, usually by baking, frying, or broiling, so that it becomes light brown.

C

Cajun descendants of French Canadians.
caramelize to turn brown and sticky when heated. This happens if the food has a sweet coating or sauce.
compote fruit cooked in a syrup.
consistency how thick or thin something is.
cordial a concentrated, sweetened fruit drink.
couscous a North African dish or crushed or coarsely ground wheat.
cream to beat butter and sugar together to add air.
crudités thin strips of raw vegetables, usually served with a dip.
crystalize to form crystals.
curdle when the liquid and solid parts of an ingredient or mixture separate. Milk curdles when overheated and cakes can curdle if the eggs are too cold or added too quickly.

D

deseed to take the seeds out.
dice to cut food into small cubes.
dissolve to melt a solid into a liquid, usually with heat.
dough a firm mixture of flour, liquid, and usually other ingredients, that can be kneaded.
drizzle to pour slowly, in a trickle.

EF

extract a concentracted essence (flavor) of a plant.
filo pastry a flaky pastry made with thin sheets of dough.
fondue a dish in which small pieces of food are dipped in a large pot of sauce.
freezerproof made to withstand being frozen, without cracking or breaking.

GH

ganache an icing or filling made from chocolate and heavy cream.

grate to use a grater to make thin shreds of a food.

grease to spread a thin layer of butter or oil to stop food from sticking to the pan.

griddle to cook food over heat on a special ridged pan that makes black lines.

guacamole a Mexican dip made from avocadoes.

heatproof made to withstand heat without cracking or breaking.

IJK

ingredients the different foods that are added together to make a dish.

knead to fold and press dough with your hands to make it smooth and stretchy.

LM

liquify to blend or process a food until it is liquid.

marinate to soak food in a sauce to add flavor.

mash to crush food like bananas or boiled potatoes to make a smooth mixture.

mix to put ingredients together and stir them.

moderate average, or in the middle.

NOP

nonstick coated with a substance that prevents food from sticking.

nutrition things in food that nourish the body.

ovenproof made to withstand the heat of an oven without cracking or breaking.

pesto an Italian sauce made from pine nuts, cheese, and herbs.

pith the white layer underneath the skin of a citrus fruit.

pulp the soft matter left over when water is squeezed from fruit or vegetables.

purée to blend or liquidize food.

QRS

quantity how much of something there is.

season to add salt and pepper to enhance flavor.

salsa a spicy Mexican relish of chopped mixed vegetables, usually with tomatoes, onions, and chilies.

shallow fry to fry in about 1/2 in (1 cm) of oil, so that the outside turns golden and crispy.

sift to shake food through a strainer to remove lumps.

simmer to bubble gently below or just at boiling point.

starter a smaller dish, served as a first course before the main course.

stir fry to fry food in a little oil over a high heat, stirring constantly.

sterilize to destroy bacteria and germs, usually with boiling water.

stock a flavored liquid in which meat, fish, or vegetables are cooked.

strain to use a strainer to drain a liquid.

sundae a dish of ice cream served with a topping usually made of fruit, nuts, and syrup.

TUV

tofu a soft cheeselike food prepared from soybean milk.

vegetarian someone who doesn't eat meat.

volume how much of something there is.

WXYZ

wok a large bowl-shaped pan, used for stir frying.

whip/whisk to beat into a froth using a whisk or fork, to add air.

zest the outer peel of a citrus fruit, used as a flavoring.

Index